I0473663

THE APT PRINCIPLE:

The Business Plan That You Carry in Your Head

BY RUSSELL F. MORAN

Coddington Press
PO Box 419
East Islip, NY 11730

Printed in the United States of America
ISBN-10: 1468010433
EAN-13: 9781468010435

Library of Congress Control Number: 2011962092
CreateSpace, North Charleston, SC

To all of my employers, employees, clients, and customers over the years, all of whom provided the insights upon which this book is based.

Contents

Acknowledgements

I thank my good friend and editor, Nick Wartella, for his keen eye, his insight, and his discipline over my sometimes quirky punctuation. I also thank my wife Lynda, an editor for many years, for her sharp, yet polite, criticisms. Her input was invaluable.

Introduction

A business plan is a formal document setting forth the goals of a business and how those goals can be met. But business plans are often not written; and if they are written, they are often forgotten. Any business owner or manager will recognize the truth in that statement. The problem is that business planning is a time-consuming process and even when the business plan is complete, it is a task to keep referring to it. What is missing in most business plans is the mental aspect, an easy-to-remember set of principles that has become part of one's thinking— a core set of guidelines.

Business plans are not written for someone else, although it may be required by a third party, especially a potential lender or investor. A business plan must be written by *you, for yourself.* Too often people think of a business plan as something that they have to do, not something from which they will derive a direct benefit. Nothing could be farther from the truth. A well-executed business plan is the most important document in your organization, and it should guide every decision that you make. But keep in mind that an important document that is not constantly referred to and updated may as well never have been written.

The APT Principle tackles this problem—the lack of a plan or the ignoring of a plan—and inserts into the planning process the most important missing element: a paperless set of guidelines that you always carry with you— in your head.

CHAPTER 1

The APT Principle

There are three kinds of business people in the world: those who have a business plan, those who don't and don't care, and those who don't have a plan but at least feel bad about it.

If you fail to plan, you plan to fail. That oft-quoted phrase isn't quoted often enough. A business without a plan is a rudderless enterprise that lurches from situation to situation, sometimes seizing opportunities, but often missing them. It is a business that heads in a wrong direction because there is no coherent set of ideas to keep it focused, no organizing principle to provide guidance. A banker or investor won't give you a glance if you don't have a plan, and for good reason. Nobody wants to put money at risk if there is no clear direction for a business. Even if you are not looking for capital, a business plan is the most crucial step in the beginning of your business. During the dot-com bubble of the mid-to-late 1990s, having a business plan was considered optional. All you needed was an *idea,* and the technological rocket called the Internet would take care of the rest. I recall visiting a sprawling building nearby once known as the Long Island Technology Center, an amazing and exciting rabbit warren of small start-up companies looking to make it in the New Economy. Formerly a building owned by defense contractor Northrop Grumman, it underwent a $24 million renovation in 1999. Each office was wired with the most sophisticated gadgetry available, and only technology-related companies could apply for a lease. The place had an aura about it, a palpable sense that big things were about to happen. When I chatted with a few of the owners, I noticed one thing they all had in common: a belief in the sacredness of *the idea*. Everybody wanted to get in on the fun. The place still exists twelve years later, but the focus is no longer strictly on technology companies; it is now known as the Long Island Business and Technology Small Business Development Center. The dot-com bubble had burst, and with it many of those little companies driven by ideas only. Ideas create businesses, but a business run by ideas alone is a bad idea.

I recall Lawrence Taylor, the New York Giants football great and budding entrepreneur. After he retired from the gridiron, he looked for business opportunities. How is this for a great idea? Sell clothing over the Internet with Lawrence Taylor's name on it. The newspapers were abuzz with reports on the endeavor. Okay, L.T. How? And to whom? What is the business model? Those were the days! Back then it was the idea that mattered.

Don't get me wrong—ideas are critical, and some of the most inspiring stories in American entrepreneurialism came from a simple idea. How about holding auctions online (eBay) or developing a website where friends could meet online and exchange information (Facebook). Or, what about a search engine that based results on the popularity of the returned results (Google) or starting a company that would write software for the newly invented personal computer (Microsoft). What about a personal computer with a graphical interface that made things easier on the user (Apple's Macintosh). Ideas have power, and ideas always come first. But to bring ideas into the sunshine, and to yield a profit, the ideas need to be anchored with a plan.

Planning should never be drudgery; it's where you awaken your dreams, jog your brain, add content to your thoughts, and mix a little concrete into your wild hopes. Planning is inspiring, exciting, uplifting, and just plain fun. You should hold it that way. If you think of planning as a task to be avoided, your first job is to check your **attitude.** It needs adjusting! You need to commit to the idea that planning is something exciting, something that you love, and something that never stops. Imagine beginning a boat trip without charting a course, which is a nautical way of saying *creating a plan.* All you have is the idea. "Let's go to…" How, exactly, do you get there? How long will it take? How much fuel do you need? How much water and provisions should you have aboard? If you have a problem, where are the towing services along the way? Ignore these questions, which means ignore the job of planning, and your life could be at risk. I owned a trawler named *Andiamo*, which is Italian for "Let's go." My wife and I used to love to do just that, but never without a plan.

The problem with a business plan, and the reason why so many neglect to write one, is that even though it is exciting and fun, it is a challenging mental exercise—one that requires clear thinking, diligence, and consultation with your advisors, especially your accountant. An even bigger problem is that once the plan is done, you have a feeling of *mission accomplished,* so you put the finished product into a drawer and forget about it. Big mistake. Part of your plan should be a scheduled calendar entry to review the plan periodically. It should be treated as an important meeting that you can't put off. Over the years I have served on many not-for-profit boards. One thing I noticed about most of these organizations was that they all had a long-range plan—but it was never discussed at board meetings.

Having a plan, without *following* the plan, is like having food and forgetting to eat it.

Business Plan Avoidance

Business plan avoidance—the failure to write one or the failure to follow one—is a reality for too many businesses. It's always easier to handle matters as they show up. As the old saying goes, when you're up to your ass in alligators, it's easy to forget that your objective is to drain the swamp. Writing a business plan, or consulting one that has been written, takes you away from the day-to-day activities that any business requires. It takes conscious effort. It's like exercise: If you don't work out today, you're not going to suddenly turn into an overweight wheezing slob (not today anyway). But if you continue to avoid exercise, your health will eventually show it. Being distracted by the day-to-day necessities of running a business is actually a way of plan avoidance. Digging into the daily minutia of business can be a calming exercise for those who wish to avoid the big picture. This is especially dangerous for a business when things are going well because the pleasant hum of good times will mask structural business problems that may lurk beneath the smooth cash flow and profits. Diving into the details *seems like work,* but it isn't, at least not for a manager or owner of the business. Here is an important distinction to always keep in mind: there is a difference between working *in* your business and working *on* your business. If you fail to keep that distinction in front of you, you will dedicate your business life to performing the chores of an entry level clerk.

The APT Principle – The Cure for Business Plan Avoidance

Everything—*EVERYTHING*—that happens to your business, both good and bad, is a function of one of these three things: **attitude, practice,** or **technology,** and any problem or opportunity can be focused like a laser by determining which of these three categories fits the situation. This is the *APT Principle.* It is a diagnostic tool, a thought organizer, an attention focuser. It is the business plan that *you carry in your head.* Think of the *APT Principle* not only as a component of your business plan, but also as its guiding standard. Do not think of the *APT Principle* as a nice idea you get from reading this book, a good concept that maybe, someday, you will get around to implementing. When writing your formal business plan, I urge you to include the *APT Principle* in every part of it. You should internalize it and make it a part of your automatic thought process. Unless you lose your head, the *APT Principle* is with you all the time.

Attitude

This is not a lecture about keeping a positive attitude, but a positive attitude sure beats the hell out of a negative one. No, **attitude** means a lot more than just keeping positive. We are all products of zillions of sensory inputs from the moment of birth. Our fears, our joys, our sorrows—our lives—are functions of all of these fleeting instances, mainly the ones from childhood. We have no recollection of most of these instances, but they are filed away in our subconscious whether we like it or not. A psychotherapist's job is to help people locate the origins of these thoughts and to bring them up in the present and deal with them. A healthy mental life requires that we be aware that much of who we are is beneath the surface of conscious thought. We think of these as preconceived notions. This is not stuff that you analyze and then make decisions based on the analysis. These notions are just there; they are, well, preconceived. Did you ever notice that some people just piss you off from the moment you meet them and you can't find a rational explanation for it? Ovid, the great Roman poet, hit the nail on the head: *"Non amo te, Sabidi; nec possum dicere quare; hoc tantum possum dicere: non amo te."* (I don't like you, Sabidi, and I can't say why; this only can I say: I don't like you). Are there any Sabidis in your life, people who you just don't like, and don't know why? Cut them some slack; they probably had nothing to do with your preconceived hang-up. It's much healthier to recognize that this person you just met and suddenly dislike probably reminds your deep unconscious of some nasty bastard who did you wrong. Maybe it was a schoolyard bully, a harsh teacher, or an unreasonable boss. Let's face it, even though you may own your own business or practice, you don't have the luxury of dealing only with people who appeal to you. There are times when you have to work with a person you find unlikeable. Let's take a look at a few preconceived notions that can get in our way:

Fears: dogs, cats, heights, darkness, thunder, a ringing phone, etc. Simply recognizing that we have certain fears gives us some control over them and helps us avoid counterproductive rationalization. I have a thing about heights. Back when I practiced law, I once had a court call at the New York State Court of Claims, which was located on one of the upper floors of the late World Trade Center. As I approached the bench to confer with the judge, he looked at me and said, "Counselor, are you feeling okay?" I guess my green color indicated that I didn't care to do business in the clouds. But simply by recognizing that I had this issue made it easier to deal with. No, dogs are not out to get you.

Likes: technical things, people, running, reading, etc. Different strokes for different folks. Do you love to get into details, or do you prefer that someone else give you an executive overview? Knowing what you like can impact your planning, delegating, and executing. It is always an opportunity for an **attitude** check when you find yourself doing something you like, because it may be unimportant and a tremendous waste of time. A lot of people like Twitter or Facebook; I do. But do you ever find yourself thinking, "Where did the last two hours go?"

Dislikes: meetings, complaining customers, employees' mistakes, etc. It's very important to recognize things that you don't like, as poor unlikeable Sabidi in the example above. Once you recognize this, your recognition alone will eliminate some of the power it has over you. Don't psychoanalyze it, obsess about it, or subject yourself to mind-fucking (as some vulgarians from the 1970s would say). If you don't like pickles, you don't like pickles. What's to analyze?

I'm not trying to put Dr. Phil out of a job here. My purpose is to emphasize that a lot of our **attitudes** are just there, and they exist without any conscious choosing on our part. It is crucial to recognize this because here is the bad news: sometimes, many times, *you have to change your attitude.* That's right—consciously change your mind. We usually think of changing our mind as the equivalent of "I just don't feel that way anymore." No, I'm talking about a *conscious decision* to change. For example, let's say you have an important project that you are working on with five of your employees. You notice that there is a communication problem, with endless e-mails back and forth, many of which show that certain team members do not understand parts of the project. So, you use the *APT Principle* to diagnose the problem. You rule out technology issues and determine that there is a problem with **attitude** (yours or theirs) and possibly a **practice** concern as well. You realize that all of the communication snafus could be corrected by a meeting or two, bringing the whole team together where they can ask as well as tell—something that calls for synchronous (back and forth), rather than asynchronous (one way) communication. You then realize that your *hatred of meetings* is what is causing the problem. There are all kinds of upsets going on, and the team members are pissed off with each other and with you, simply because you have this dumb, stubborn hatred of meetings. You conclude that it is a good **practice** to schedule regular team meetings to keep the project moving. You still don't like meetings, but the *APT Principle* gives you the diagnostic framework to realize that sometimes you have to do things that you don't like. When your **attitude** gets in the way, it's time to change your attitude, or at least recognize that you are causing the problem. The alternative is to blame everything else for the issue and waste time trying to solve the wrong problem.

Think of your **attitude** as the foundation of a building. A bad attitude, like a bad foundation, will ultimately result in a pile of rubble. I have visited countless businesses over the years and I can assure you, some were piles of rubble, and some were soon to become so. A positive attitude is not just something for salespeople and talk show hosts; it is the basis of a rewarding life as well as a rewarding business. It determines how you build your business, how you relate to clients, customers, employees, and other business people. It determines how you'll respond to the inevitable problems that occur and what steps you'll take to correct them. It *creates* the dynamic between you and all those around you. A positive attitude is for all those who wish to build a successful life. It is for you. By a positive attitude I don't mean putting on blinders and pretending that everything is always a bright spring day. I once sat next to a guy at a Rotary meeting who was our guest speaker that day. He billed himself as a "positive thinking coach" and was so focused on his premise that he had a whole weird list of things that he wouldn't do, so as not to muss up his attitude. He bragged, "I never read newspapers, watch, or listen to the news. If there is negativity out there, I keep it away from me." This guy wasn't just a positive thinker, he was a positive jerk. If positive thinking means avoiding reality, it never would have caught on. Serious, grown-up positive thinking means thinking in a way that serves your life, rather than defeating it. It means that when you encounter something that reality tells you is not a good thing, you confront it, acknowledge it, and handle it. Werner Erhard, the legendary founder of the *est* training, the wildly popular self-help seminar in the '70s and '80s, once said something I will never forget. When he encountered something that was objectively bad—a flat tire, a broken air conditioner, an empty gas tank—he would always say to himself, "Okay, I got it." Now that's powerful, that's positive, that's a grown-up way to encounter a difficult situation. It is a simple acknowledgement of reality as it shows up. You don't deny the reality, but you don't add to it a lot of negative garbage that will only make it worse. By saying, "Okay, I got it," you commit yourself to simply handling the problem. You don't crawl into your head and say stuff like, "I should have checked that tire" or "Why does this crap always happen to me?" or "My day is now ruined." Instead, it is much better to say, "Okay, I got it." Get it?

Practices: Best Practices

Best practices, in the business sense, are those proce-dures, guidelines, and rules that make a business stand out. Note that the phrase is *best* practices, not *good* or *better,* but BEST. Rather than reinventing the wheel every day, a good manager will institute practices that handle the running of a business. Best practices are like oil to a motor; without it the engine seizes up and your vehicle slows to a stop—a very long stop. Without best practices, a business can seize up just like a car engine. Employees love best practices because it helps them perform their jobs more efficiently and with the knowledge that what they are doing makes sense. Don't overlook employee pride. Nobody wants to work for a sloppy company where the workers constantly have to apologize to customers because customer dissatisfaction reflects directly on them. Customers absolutely love best practices because it makes them fond of your business and makes them want to give you more business. Let's look at a few best practices that any business should, well, *practice.*

- Write a business plan, and set a regular calendar entry to review it.
- Provide constant and regular employee training.
- Have structured and predictable human resources procedures so that employees know what is expected of them and what they can expect from you.
- Provide telephone training for all employees, especially in etiquette.
- Deal with customer complaints, institute guidelines, and train employees on customer service.
- Develop a filing system, with an emphasis on *system.* If a key employee leaves, it shouldn't take you a year to figure out how he or she filed things. Filing should not be left to personal whim. Filing is discussed in detail in Chapter 14.
- Meet deadlines, especially when customers are involved.

- Have a disaster plan. Could your business survive a week without electricity?
- Pay bills on time. Good credit is a basic need for any business.
- Send birthday and anniversary cards to customers.
- Have a website, with changing content, and update it frequently.
- Collect receivables with a structured, efficient procedure.
- Use the *APT Principle* as a regular part of your day.

The above list could go on forever. There are dozens if not hundreds of additional practices for a manufacturing company, for example. The point is, you should constantly look for areas where you can put a best practice in place. NOTE: In the many standard business plan templates I have seen, I haven't encountered one where best practices was a separate entry. I suggest that you make it a part of your formal plan. Use my list above and tailor it to your needs.

Technology: A Brief History of the Past 30 Years

When I began my publishing company over 30 years ago, we actually prepared our weekly reports for *The New York Jury Verdict Reporter* with a *typewriter*. I would write or dictate the report, give it to my secretary, who would then type it. Redoing a typo after the paper was taken out of the machine was a nightmare. A lot of people reading this book probably have never seen a real typewriter—only those in movies or museums. Typewriters survived well into the personal computer revolution for the sole function of filling in paper forms. That, thank God, has gone away with the advent of easy-to-use online forms and scanners. Our phone system, of course, was AT&T, known simply as The Phone Company. When I was on the road, I always made sure to carry around a lot of change in case I needed to make a call from a phone booth. I kind of miss that old familiar smell of urine! *Cell phone* was not yet in the dictionary, nor was it in our imaginations. Wireless landline phones were the most exciting development in years. My appointment calendar, address book, and things-to-do list were all carried in my trusty paper Day-Timer appointment book. Smartphone? Whazzat? When I needed to get a document to somebody fast, I would use a courier service or have one of my employees deliver it. It was about seven years after I started my company that I even heard of a fax machine. I bought my first fax machine in 1983 for $2,000. Now, faxing is almost obsolete. Simply scan a document and e-mail it as an attachment. Indeed, when we look back, the last few decades almost seem like the Dark Ages.

Then, Bill Gates, Steve Jobs, and assorted other geniuses came along and changed the world. It was still a rocky road in the early 1980s, even as the personal computer revolution took off. Anyone who ever used MS-DOS (Microsoft Disk Operating System), the pre-Windows disk operating system, knows the meaning of frustration. Accidently hit *Control F* and your entire hard drive got wiped out. I remember my first hard drive in 1984. It weighed about 30 pounds, cost $2,500, and held a massive 15 megabytes. Now, a tiny flash drive can hold 16 gigabytes, over 16,000 times the storage of my old hard drive, and it goes for under $20. Each of our staff would back up that day's work onto floppy disks at the end of the day. It took an average of 12 disks per employee. But, even in its infancy, the technology revolution provided enormous new options for people—and especially for business.

Next came the game changer of all time: the Internet. Although originally developed in the 1960s as Arpanet (Advanced Research Projects Agency net) by the United States Department of Defense, the Internet became popular with the masses in the early 1990s with the web browser Mosaic, which later became Netscape. Finding stuff in the early days of the Internet was a challenge, only a little better than looking things up on paper. Real live editors would put content into massive directories with deep layers; this was what Yahoo! brought to the game. Although faster, it was a cumbersome and time-consuming task to look up something. Then, in 1998, a paradigm shift occurred—Google, the mother of all search engines. Using complex mathematical algorithms, which ranked a website's relevance by the number of pages that linked back to the original site, Google quickly became a verb, as well as a wildly successful corporation. Now, if you need information on something, you *Google* it.

Ten years from now, what I have written above will appear quaint. In Chapter 14, I discuss how modern technology can perform magic for your business.

A Note on Winning

Red Auerbach, the great coach and general manager of the Boston Celtics from 1950 to 1984 was asked in a post-game interview, "Why do the Celtics have such a great record of winning?" I will never forget his response: "It's not the fancy plays or brilliant strategy. My guys know how to dribble and shoot." In other words, it is the *fundamentals*. In his 34 years as general manager, the Celtics won 16 NBA titles. As a coach, he had 1,037 victories against 548 losses. The man was a winner.

The goal of playing a sport is to win, and the same is true in business. I have played on winning teams, and I have played on losing teams; I have worked for winning companies, as well as for losers. There are few simple facts in this complicated life, but here is one of them: it's much better to win!

What You Should Expect from This Book

My goal is for your business to become not only a source of significant wealth but also a vehicle of great personal satisfaction and enrichment. I want your business to be a place that you can't wait to go to in the morning. I want to replace the headache, the stomach pain, and the unconscious facial twitch with a calm smile. I want you to profit, but I also want you to have a well-earned sense of pride for what you have done and what you are doing. That's what *I* want.

What Do *You* Want?

"What do *you* want?" is perhaps the most important question in this entire book. Unless you get clear on that question, this book will be nothing more than a reading exercise. I will help you, but you need to put yourself in the picture. In the ensuing chapters, we will discuss writing a mission statement, developing a business plan, writing a marketing plan, goal setting, time management, and a host of other topics. But, unless you internalize the processes and inject yourself into it, those processes will only be words. What do *you* want?

Reading this book requires your active participation; it is not a typical passive reading endeavor. More specifically, I need you to adopt, from time to time, a way of thinking, a mind-shift, if you will, away from *you* the reader and toward someone who is far more important: your client or customer. It is a matter of **attitude**. If you want this book to have a serious impact on your business or professional practice, you must keep this customer focus constantly in mind. A useful mental game is to literally picture yourself *on the other side of the desk* as you are envisioning the events unfold. What I am really asking you to do is what modern management theorists, from Peter Drucker to Tom Peters, have been espousing for years: *Become customer focused.* You may substitute the word "client" for "customer," but I suggest the following: consider the two words synonymous for the purposes of this book. I make this suggestion because it will be easy for you to visualize yourself as a client when you think of yourself as customer. In the next chapter, the customer-focused philosophy is expanded, along with practical tools to put the philosophy into effect.

The Two Reasons to Be in Business

Bob Shearer, my business coach for many years, believed in fundamentals. When I first met him, he said to me, "There are only two reasons to be in business: to have fun and to make money—in equal proportions." Over the years he would constantly remind me of this. You can't have fun if you're not making money, and you can't make money if you're not having fun.

I invite you to keep these two reasons in mind as you read this book. So, have fun…and make money!

Oh yes, I almost left something out. When YOU dribble and shoot well, YOU score!

Chapter 1 Summary

In this chapter I discussed the following:
- An introduction to the *APT Principle*
- The cure for business plan avoidance
- **Attitude:** fears, likes, and dislikes
- **Practices:** a list of best practices
- **Technology:** the last 30 years and what it means
- What you should expect from this book
- Two Reasons to be in Business: to have fun and to make money

CHAPTER 2

Shifting Your Mind to the Business of Business

APT Principle: Attitude

A Word about Money and Your Attitude

I must put in a word for those of you who solemnly believe that the idea of making money is somehow beneath you, that your interest is not to earn money but only to serve people and society. You are quite happy with your 1969 Volvo, your two threadbare suits, and your humble office. That's fine by me. If you happen to make some money following the lessons of this book, please give it away or, better yet, send it to me. I promise to put it to good use. But please read on! Service to others is a noble goal and one to which I heartily subscribe. If it is your *only* goal, and you wish to deflect the dollars that might come your way, you nevertheless must observe the fundamentals of business—even if your sole objective is service.

Profit: It's Your Job

Profit is not some arcane principle lost in the language of accountancy. Boiled down to its bare essentials, profit means that after you paid for the goods you bought or assembled to sell, and after all the expenses, there is money left over, which can be distributed to the owners.

It's your job to make a profit. That's right. It's your job, not a by-product of your efforts, but a requirement in the game of business. If you don't make a profit, you break even; or worse, you suffer a loss. If you suffer a loss, who pays for it? You? Your customers? Your suppliers and vendors? Your bank? Taxpayers? Somebody pays when you suffer a loss. As Milton Friedman said, "There is no free lunch." So much for the obvious. What might not be so obvious is that profit helps everyone who has contact with your business—your employees, your customers, your vendors, your banker, and of course, yourself. Profit means good credit; profit means the ability to amass cash reserves; profit means the ability to seize opportunities when they arise without scrounging for cash; profit means the ability to charge the customer a reasonable price; and profit means the ability to lend a helping hand when you see it's needed. Andrew Carnegie or Bill Gates didn't give away zillions of dollars by being unprofitable. Profit also means the ability to reap the personal financial rewards of your business, to build a better life for you and your family.

If you are a not-for-profit entity, you cannot make a profit, which is distributed to owners; but you still need to bring in revenues in excess of your expenses. What is left over goes into more of the programs and activities that fulfill the mission of the not-for-profit organization. If your not-for-profit enterprise loses money, who pays? Here's who: your vendors whose invoices are ignored, your employees who lose their jobs and, all too often, the taxpayer. A good not-for-profit manager looks at the enterprise exactly the way a for-profit firm does. Good business practices are not just for business people.

The Free Market: How it Serves Us

A socialist wants government to deliver *social value,* believing that such a noble thing cannot be left in the hands of greedy capitalists. Consider this: a business *does deliver social value.* Food is certainly a social value; it is also a necessity of life. The next time you go to a supermarket, observe the bewildering array of choices in front of you. Compare this to the reality of food stores in the old Soviet Union. A person would have to wait in line for hours just to pick out a couple of onions. In Cuba, where 85 percent of the people work for the government, the average salary is $20 per month. It's good that the benevolent government provides free health care because with such lousy nutrition that $20 a month provides, one needs it. The Cuban government even has a specific list of enterprises that it allows private citizens to indulge in. With the government's blessing, you can even embark on a private career as a bed frame repairman. I'm not kidding. Cuba recently began to expand the list of jobs that can be performed in the private sector, mainly because its economy is a festering carcass, especially since the collapse of its patron, the Soviet Union. A society dedicated to the redistribution of wealth is based on the view of human nature that private individuals need to be controlled and cannot be trusted to deliver the goods and services that a society needs. The motivations that we take for granted in a free society are suppressed in a totalitarian socialist state. In a free enterprise society, on the other hand, people are motivated to get ahead in life, to seek advancement and, yes, to make more money. *Soviet Man,* the mythical character of the old Soviet ideology, the man who was to be motivated to provide his best efforts for the good of all, never showed up. Recall the dark joke of the communist era: "They pretend to pay us; we pretend to work."

The reason your local supermarket is awash in such a wide array of choices is that somebody is making a buck. Someone profits from providing nutritious food; someone profits by providing choices; and someone profits from getting the food to market in a timely manner. The greedy capitalists who stock our supermarkets know a little secret: the better they serve us, the greater their profit because we want to visit their stores and buy their products. The better you run your business, the more clients and customers you can serve. And the better you will serve them. Show me a well-functioning government agency, and I will show you an agency that is run like a business. The same is true for not-for-profit organizations. If you wish, you can change my suggestion that you *have fun and make money* into *have fun and bring in revenue*. Think of money as the blood of your organization: run low on it, and you get sick and die. That is NOT fun.

The Lead Pencil is Impossible to Make

The following is based on a classic essay written by Leonard E. Read in 1958 entitled "I, Pencil: My Family Tree as Told to Leonard E. Read." Let's follow the pencil as it is made. The pencil begins its journey to becoming a writing instrument with cedar, grown perhaps in northern California or Oregon. The loggers, cutters, fabricators, and road clearers all use countless pieces of equipment, all manufactured by somebody. The logs are shipped to a mill in San Leandro California, on rail trains or flatbed trucks. The timber is cut into small, pencil-sized pieces of wood. Once at the pencil factory, multimillion dollar machines go to work. Each slat is given eight grooves by a complex machine, after which another machine lays the "lead" in every other slat, applies glue, and places another slat atop—a lead sandwich, so to speak. The lead is really graphite and comes from Ceylon, and it is mixed with clay from Mississippi. Then wetting agents are added and, after passing through numerous machines, the mixture finally appears as endless extrusions—as from a sausage grinder—cut to size, dried, and baked for several hours at 1,850°F. To increase their strength and smoothness, the lead is then treated with a hot mixture, which includes wax from Mexico—paraffin and hydrogenated natural fats. The cedar receives six coats of lacquer. The metal ferrule is what holds the eraser and is made of brass. After that the eraser is added, made of ingredients from the Dutch East Indies and pumice from Italy.

The amazing thing about the simple lead pencil is that no single person makes it, nor even directs how it is made. Countless miners, woodsmen, truck drivers, shippers, and metal fabricators from all over the world are involved in its raw materials and its manufacturing. It is the classic example of the "invisible hand" of capitalism at work. No central planning committee could possibly accomplish such a task as making a lead pencil. The entire essay can be viewed at the website of the

Library of Economics and Liberty: http://www.econlib.org/library/Essays/rdPncl1.html. I suggest that you print it out and give it to each of your kids. Better yet, send it to their teachers.

Consider Microsoft. Recall Bill Gates and Paul Allen at that famous historical moment in Harvard Square. They realized from a magazine article about the Altair computer—the first personal computer—that a revolution was about to begin; and they could make a fortune from it by writing the software to make it work. They saw this, as only a couple of whiz kids can, as an opportunity of a lifetime. Did they start Microsoft to serve you and me? Your first inclination would be to say, no, they did it to make money. But let's take a look at what really happened. To earn its wild profits over the years, Gates and his team at Microsoft realized that the road to success was to serve the people who needed its products, which included almost everybody. Microsoft, with programs such as Word (with which I am writing this book), Excel, PowerPoint, Outlook, and other Microsoft Office suite products, has done an amazing thing: it created a standard, a standard that makes all our lives easier. When discussing computing matters with employees or colleagues, we are mostly on the same page. How do you do this or that in Word? Just turn to the person next to you, who also uses Word. Now to be clear, the folks at Microsoft didn't perform these miracles out of compassion for us computer users. No, they did it to make money. But they realized, as any successful business realizes, that the way to make money is to serve people. As the great economist Milton Friedman said, "The most important single central fact about a free market is that no exchange takes place unless both parties benefit." Free enterprise is a marvelous system.

A Word about Fun and Your Attitude

No, I'm not talking about taking time off for golf or sailing, although your leisure time is extremely important to your overall well-being and will help your business by keeping your **attitude** in positive mode. What I am talking about here is to actually *have fun at the business of business*. Fun doesn't always involve smiling or laughter. Fun is that way of being when things are simply going the right way, when you are making things happen and not at the mercy of whatever shows up. Having fun can mean working on a new advertising campaign or enjoying the results of a campaign that was well executed. Having fun can even mean working on a business plan. Having fun means *enjoying* what you are doing. But it can also mean the traditional understanding of fun: smiling and laughing.

Please don't misunderstand the notion of fun. A business is not necessarily supposed to be a big happy family, at least not as a business objective. Jack Welch, the legendary CEO of General Electric, was known as Jack the Knife. Although he did not have a tyrannical personality, he communicated to every executive that his or her job was to make a success of GE and, if they didn't hit their goals, they would be fired. Everyone knew where he stood. The fun of working for a guy like Jack Welch included knowing that you were expected to perform, or else. If your business does appear to be a big happy family, it should be a by-product of your well-run organization, one that is properly infused with the right **attitudes, practices,** and **technology.**

Have fun!

Chapter 2 Summary

In this chapter I discussed the following:

- Money and your attitude toward it. Even a not-for-profit organization needs revenues in excess of expenses.
- Making a profit is your job; it's not optional.
- The free market and how it serves us.
- How to make a lead pencil.
- Fun—the kind of fun that means enjoying your business.

CHAPTER 3

Becoming Customer Focused

APT Principles: Attitude and Practices

Put yourself in a customer's shoes. Think of the various businesses that you interact with as a customer: the dry cleaner, supermarket, copier repair company, landscaper, service station, barber or beauty salon, credit card company, overnight delivery company, electrician, plumber, carpenter, TV cable company, computer repair company, auto repair shop, software vendor, restaurant and diner, delicatessen, office supply company, veterinarian, dentist, doctor, lawyer, telephone company, janitorial service company, painter, hotel and resort, airline, limo service, and so on. You will notice that this list is random, and it is by no means all-inclusive. The reason I listed so many is simple: they are my partners in writing this book. That's right! They are my partners because, as you read this book, I want you to constantly think about anyone with whom you do business. Think about your relationship with them. Think of all the positive and negative encounters you've had as learning experiences for interactions with your own customers and clients. Observe how you feel when you receive good service or bad service. I have no doubt that as you read through the list above that you had an opinion, whether consciously expressed or merely a gut feeling, about each of the businesses or professions. Some of your random thoughts might have included something like the following:

Overnight delivery company—"Great people. I wish everyone was so helpful and efficient."

Copier repair company—"When my lease ends, I would use pencil rubbings before I hired them again."

Janitorial service company—"Couldn't be better—polite, competent, and reasonably priced."

Office supply company—"Not very pleasant or efficient; as soon as they have good competition, they're history."

Computer repair company—"#%@%@&*%$(@&**!"

Here's the scary news, or maybe the good news: if *you* were on the above list, your clients would have some definite opinions about you. Ensuring those opinions are nothing but positive is what this book is all about. Keeping customer relationships constantly in mind will enable you to do the mind-shift essential for reaping the rewards of this book. This customer-focused philosophy is woven throughout the book; it is the bedrock upon which a successful business is built, the foundation for any lasting plan. Building a customer-centered organization is a constant interplay of **attitude**, **practices**, and **technology**.

It's not a "Sale"—it's a Relationship

When you foster a *relationship* of trust with your customer, that customer then becomes a non-commissioned salesperson for your business. You should view a transaction with a client or customer as one of hundreds or thousands of potential transactions over time. I am constantly amazed that some business people believe that they have to profit on every sale. A couple of years ago, I purchased a new cell phone for my wife as a gift. There was one problem: it didn't work. She couldn't make or receive calls, which made the cell phone as useful as a pet rock. When I brought it back to the retailer, he tried the phone. It didn't work. It was the last model in stock, so he decided that he would simply return my money, except for a "$30 restocking fee." Why, I inquired, would he "restock" something that didn't work, and why should I pay any kind of a fee for a product that was simply useless? Because, he patiently told me, he would have to incur an expense in shipping it back to the manufacturer, as if that was a problem that I should be concerned with. A brief note to my credit card company resulted in a credit back to me for the $30; so, not only did he not get his "restocking fee," but he also lost any possibility of getting me as a regular customer. It was so important to him that he squeeze some success out of that transaction that he destroyed any chance of establishing a customer relationship with me. I'm sure you have encountered incidents of this strange phenomenon: win the transaction, lose the customer.

Legendary Customer Service

You're probably thinking, as you read the word "legendary," that I am engaging in a bit of hyperbole. I am not. Let me give you an example of how excellent service has a way of becoming legendary, sometimes in the simplest of ways. My wife and I were having breakfast at a diner a few months ago. Apparently, the hostess forgot to tell the waitress that she had seated us, and we had to wait over ten minutes before we even got coffee. I got up from my seat, went to the hostess and asked if she had forgotten us. She immediately apologized and brought us the coffee herself. She did not make excuses about how busy they were. She simply apologized. And when we were presented with the check, the hostess grabbed it from the waitress, saying, "This is on me." I grabbed it back and said, "Please, it was an honest mistake, and you made up for it." The diner was the Peter Pan Diner in Bay Shore, New York. The food is good, the service is good, and if there is an occasional slip-up, they make up for it. Notice what happened. Not only did I insist on paying, but I was so impressed with the polite offer that I even mentioned the name of the diner in this book. Another positive and recent experience I had with excellent customer service involved a local mechanic. After the umpteenth heavy snowfall on Long Island in the winter of 2010–2011, I backed my new car into a frozen snowdrift. I immediately started having trouble with all sorts of rattles and dashboard warnings. I took it to my local car repair place, where a mechanic put the car up on a lift and discovered that one of the tailpipes was twisted off its hangers. After about fifteen minutes of carefully maneuvering the pipe back in place, he took it down from the lift. "How much?" I asked the manager. "Nothing," he said. "It was no big deal." No big deal? Fifteen minutes of muscle power combined with his employee's knowledge of how to fix the problem, and he didn't think it was a big deal! His name is Ken Guercio of Guercio's Auto & Truck Repair in Islip, New York.

Ken knows something about being customer focused, and he knows how to concentrate on the relationship, not the transaction. I can't imagine using a different car repair place. By the way, I did tip the mechanic. I don't mind helping to recognize legendary customer service.

Think about experiences you have had with excellent service. You tell the story to others, don't you? And when we tell stories to friends, these stories have a way of being embellished over time. A legend is born!

I saw dramatic proof of this when I was in the legal publishing business. VerdictSearch was a research service that was part of *The New York Jury Verdict Reporter*, our main publication. It was, and still is, a service heavily relied on by trial lawyers for obtaining copies of verdict reports, especially on expert witnesses, so that attorneys use it to gather information prior to cross-examining an expert. I received a call at my home (Yes, I'm in the book.) one Sunday morning from a panicked attorney whose assistant had forgotten to order a search on a very important witness whom the attorney was to cross-examine the next day. It was a major medical malpractice case, and potentially millions of dollars were on the line. I didn't know him personally, and he got my home number from the phone book. "I know it's Sunday, but can you possibly help me out," he begged, after explaining his problem. I asked if he could wait until I finished watching "The McLaughlin Group" on TV. "Of course!" he choked. He said he would be willing to pay whatever exorbitant fee I wanted for my efforts. I told him that we never set a Sunday fee schedule, so we would just charge our usual same-day service fee. My office was 10 minutes away from my house. He needed five searches; this took me about a half hour. I was back home in time for the Jets game. I really didn't think this was a big deal. Sure, I was doing the guy a favor, but my "default-thinking" has always been to provide superior customer service, and that includes going beyond the normal call of duty. The result of this transaction was nothing short of incredible. That lawyer was so impressed with our service, he couldn't shut up about it (not that I wanted him to). I gave up counting the number of referral calls that we got from that transaction. Once, while I was speaking at a bar association seminar on legal research, the attorney I had helped happened to be there. As I was introduced to speak, he stood up in front of the audience and said loudly, "I consider it malpractice not to use Russ's service." What I had done, by that simple act of customer service, was to hire a non-commissioned salesman, an evangelist, for my business.

A similar story is told about the retail giant Walmart and its great founder, Sam Walton. One Sunday morning, a pharmacist at a Walmart store in Harrison, Arkansas, received a call from his store. A store associate informed him that one of his pharmacy customers, a diabetic, had accidentally dropped her insulin down her garbage disposal. Knowing that a diabetic without insulin could be in grave danger, the pharmacist immediately rushed to the store, opened the pharmacy, and filled the customer's insulin prescription. This is Sam Walton's "Sundown Rule." When it comes to customers, get it done—before sundown!

Sam Walton was the epitome of a business legend. Here is just one of his famous "rules" involving customer service: "Exceed your customer's expectations. If you do, they'll come back over and over. Give them what they want—and a little more. Let them know you appreciate them. Make good on all your mistakes, and don't make excuses—apologize. Stand behind everything you do. 'Satisfaction guaranteed' will make all the difference."

Sam Walton began with a variety store in rural Arkansas in 1945 and grew the enterprise to 1,720 Walmart units operating in 39 states with net sales of $43.9 billion in 1992. By 1990 Walmart was the nation's largest retailer, and still is. He is a legend, and he built this legend on customer service. One of my favorites of Sam's rules is the 10-foot Rule: whenever a customer comes within 10 feet of an employee, the employee's job is to look the customer in the eye, greet him, and ask if he needs help. I noticed that The Home Depot has borrowed a page from Sam Walton. Their employees seem to actually *want* to help you. Of course, this rule may not exactly apply to your business, unless you are in retail, but the basic idea cuts across all businesses: greet your customer or client, whether in person or on the phone, and ask if you can be of any help. Notice, once again, your own business transactions when you are on the customer side of the equation. Notice how you are willing to blab all about a business that pleases you and that you refer other customers to. You help spread legends. Now let's get others to spread *your* legend.

Dark Legends

Being legendary cuts both ways. Amazon.com's Jeff Bezos always talks about the ripple effect of getting just one customer angry, especially in the age of the Internet, where nasty stories can be told across countless forums. You must visit a website called newsucks500.com, billed as "A place where all people can get together and vent." This is a website actually dedicated to giving people a place to say all sorts of nasty things. Attacking people or companies on the Internet is called "flaming." It can be, and often is, extremely unethical, but it exists. The site also has numerous other websites pointing back to this one. Type in www.searssucks.com or www.attsucks.com and you get directed right back to newsucks500.com. Get the idea? It's getting easier and easier for people to complain about you and easier to be embarrassed. You never want to come across a website named [your business]sucks.com.

A few years ago, I purchased a gas stove to heat up a chilly room in my house. It was supposed to be delivered in two days. A week later I called to ask about its where-abouts and was abruptly told, "Sir, (Don't you love being called "sir" or "ma'am"?) you have to allow time for the paperwork to go through."

"What paperwork?" I inquired. "I bought a floor model."

"Sir," she said, "all I can tell you is that you will have it soon, as soon as the paperwork goes through."

It finally arrived a few days later. When my plumber came to hook it up, he discovered that both the temperature gauge and the gas shutoff valve were completely inoperative. Now, anybody can make a mistake. Even the Uniform Commercial Code gives a merchant time to correct an error. But behold what happened next. I called the store and advised the manager that the stove was inoperative. He said that because they were extremely busy, he would have a repairman out in about two weeks. "Two weeks!" I sputtered. "Since you just delivered a non-working stove, don't you consider this a priority?" He patiently explained to me that they were very hectic because it was their busy time of the year. Two weeks later, on the appointed day, I arranged to work at home to await the repairman. He never showed. When I called I was told that no one could appear for at least four weeks. (Of course, this was because they were "busy.") I explained my plight to American Express, which investigated, and readily credited my account. I advised the store that they could arrange to pick up the stove and present me with $95, the cost I incurred in getting it delivered. That was "against policy" I was told. So the inert piece of iron sits in our greenhouse and is used as a plant holder. My policy is not to use the names of companies that I criticize, and I won't. But to anyone I have told this story to, I consider it my civic duty to warn them about this store. Not surprisingly, I have heard similar stories from others. A dark legend, born and growing. A failure of **attitude** and **practices.**

Your sourcebook for customer service legends, good ones and dark, is with you all the time. Life is your sourcebook. Train yourself to look around and observe when you, as a customer, are being cared for or ignored, when your needs are being met, or when you are being placed on hold and forgotten. Everyone you deal with, from the auto mechanic to the diner waitress, is a source for you to learn lessons for your business. Better yet, jot down your experiences and put them into a file called "Customer Service Legends."

Bad Practices

A bad practice is one that continues to provide negative results as long as you allow it to remain in place. Now, we all do dumb things occasionally, but not usually as a conscious decision; sometimes we just screw up. When I owned my legal publishing company, I once did a direct mail campaign of about 100,000 pieces. I assumed that one of my editors had done a final proofread on the copy. That was a very dumb assumption on my part because she hadn't, and the mailing went out with a couple of embarrassing errors. When you get a solicitation from a *publisher,* the last thing you expect to see are typos. A seriously Bad Practice that I inadvertently put in place was NOT requiring a final proof to be signed off by a senior employee.

Hiring an Inexperienced Receptionist

One of the worst practices in business? Hiring the most inexperienced receptionist you can find, making sure that he or she has a very limited professional background and providing the person with no training. To make matters worse, your new receptionist lacks resourcefulness, has poor speech habits, has no sense of humor, and generally has a bad **attitude.** Do this because you can hire such a person really cheaply and save a lot of money on payroll. Voila! You have instituted a practice so bad that it can sink your business. This problem is so common in business that I'm convinced there is somebody out there teaching a seminar on this subject.

In my years in legal publishing and research, I dealt with lawyers and law firms—thousands of them. For some reason I'll never know, lawyers, in my opinion, are the worst offenders when it comes to hiring incompetent receptionists. I once called a personal injury lawyer to interview him on a case he had just tried. I didn't say the name of my company—*The New York Jury Verdict Reporter*— because some lawyers would try to duck me if they weren't pleased with the outcome of their case. So, I simply said, "Hi, this is Russ Moran. Could I please speak to Mr. Jones?" The receptionist replied (in the perfect Brooklynese twang of Marisa Tomei in the movie *My Cousin Vinny*), "He's on da phone, cudga call back layta?" "Would you like to take a message?" I inquired. "I gotta run," she said. "My boyfriend's takin' me ta lunch. Call back layta." Now, she had no idea who in the world I was. I could have been a prospective client with a million-dollar lawsuit, or another attorney about to make a generous offer on a case. Maybe I missed something in law school. I don't recall seeing in the curriculum catalog a course entitled "How to Hire a Receptionist Who Will Chase Away Clients, Cost You Money, Make Your Life Miserable, and Possibly Get You Sued for Malpractice." Okay, okay, I'm venting. But better to hear the venting from me than from one of your customers or clients.

The Good Receptionist: A Best Practice

The job of the receptionist is, for small-to-medium businesses anyway, an entry-level position. But that does not mean that it is an unimportant job. By "receptionist" I mean the person whose primary responsibility is to answer the phone, route calls, take messages, and greet visitors. In smaller organizations, the receptionist typically wears many hats. The receptionist is the voice, the personality, of your business. The first time a customer calls or walks in the office, the receptionist actually *is* your business. Of all the areas to save money, this is not one of them. How many businesses do you know of where the receptionist is hired right out of high school, where she specialized in chewing bubble gum? Think of the receptionist as your primary assistant in your goal of customer focus.

There is a theory, gaining currency, that businesses can save money by eliminating the position of receptionist. I can accept this idea only if you replace the person with a rotating *position,* reception duty so to speak. If four employees are assigned the position, make absolutely certain that each person is trained how to properly handle the job. Remember: the receptionist is the face and voice of your business.

What to Look for in a Good Receptionist

Attitude. Unless you are willing to spend a lot of money on un-training bad habits, you should look for a person with a positive disposition, a good sense of humor, and the resourcefulness to handle problems when they arise.

Skill. Unless reception is the only job that this person will be doing, good clerical and computer skills are a *must* to enable the person to multitask. Often, the receptionist is assigned projects that other employees don't have the time to do. A few examples are entering items into a database, cleaning up a database, filing, or assisting in bookkeeping duties.

Resourcefulness. Problems have a way of occurring at the worst possible time, usually when you or other managers are away from the office. A good receptionist should be able to think fast, help customers find solutions to problems, and leave customers with the feeling that they are in good hands. The most important thing that receptionists need to convey is that they take the customers' problems very seriously and that they will make sure problems are taken care of. Receptionists may not have the ability to solve the problem, but they do have the ability to let customers know that help is on the way.

How to Use the Telephone

Alexander Graham Bell invented the telephone in 1876, over 135 years ago. Judging from the way many businesses use it, one would think the phone was invented yesterday. The technology is complex, but it is a simple instrument to use, and that is the problem. Most businesses treat the telephone as a device that simply is used to receive and convey information. A major mistake!

Most large corporations recognize the importance of good telephone usage in their customer relations. Indeed, except for mail and e-mail, it is the primary way they communicate with customers. Many large companies have banks of phones manned by highly trained employees who have made telephone communications an art form. American Express and Bank of America spring to mind. I just hope that these fine people are not in BofA's layoff plans. Unfortunately, many small-to-medium businesses, and a few large ones, treat the phone as an annoyance. The following points should be communicated to any employee who uses the telephone:

Smile. Try a simple exercise. Ask another person to do it with you. Place a sheet of paper or a magazine in front of your face and repeat 10 words, each of them twice. Ask the other person if he thinks you are smiling or not when you say the words. Jot down his response with a "y" or "n." You will be amazed to find that the other person is able to tell if you are smiling at least nine out of ten times. The smile comes through even if it is not visible. It actually changes the quality of your voice, and it orally communicates to the person on the other end of the line that you are friendly.

Make the caller "feel welcome." I coached my employees to think of a caller as a long lost friend. This is a powerful visualization technique. Imagine your phone demeanor if it *was* that old friend. Now simply adopt that **attitude** with every caller. Even if you are not in a friendly mood, you don't have to go to drama school to "act friendly."

Identify yourself and your company. I hope I don't have to convince any reader that, in answering a business call, one never just says "Hello." But let's take it a bit further. Answering the phone with "XYZ Corporation" is cold and impersonal. "XYZ Corporation, how may I help you?" is better. By far, the best is "XYZ Corporation. This is Bob. How may I help you?" The caller now has the opportunity to use your first name and thereby establish a friendly transaction from the start.

Use the caller's first name. If you don't know it, ask for it. I know this is controversial, but try it. In my many years dealing with "tough customers," I became convinced that for every pompous ass that you alienate, you will make ninety-nine friends by using their first name. People, and that includes you, like to hear their first name spoken, and that includes hearing it over the telephone. Caution: I come from a North American business background, and what I just said about using first names works in this culture. In some cultures, it is considered impolite, even insulting, to use a person's first name, unless you are a very good friend or relative. This is especially true of Japanese. If the person on the other end has an accent, play it safe and use the proper greeting.

On-hold etiquette. Don't you love being put on "terminal hold"? Have you ever been on hold for so long that you forgot who you were waiting to speak to? "Holdsmanship" is a very important art for any business that wants to keep customers happy. The rule in my company was not to keep anyone hanging for more than 30 seconds without picking up the blinking line and saying,

"She's still on the phone. Would you like to continue to hold or would you prefer to leave a message?" There are numerous telecom companies that provide "on-hold messages." Why not use the on-hold time to politely pitch your products or services? This still doesn't change the rule that you must break in periodically to let the caller know that you realize that he or she is still alive.

Voicemail. This is a wonderful technology that enables a caller to leave an exact message and explain what needs to be clarified, without the danger of someone writing down the wrong information. But a caller should always be given the choice between voicemail and leaving a message with a live person. Sometimes action is required, and voicemail just won't do. Used properly, it affords good customer service and saves time and errors as well. Train your people to always say, "He's not in at the moment; can I transfer you to his voicemail?"

Handling the Irate Customer—Rules for Damage Control

Sometimes you screw up. Sometimes there is a misunderstanding between your company and your customer; sometimes your product or service doesn't work as it should; sometimes one of your employees may have been abrupt; and sometimes your customer or client may have gotten out of the wrong side of the bed that morning, and *you're* going to pay for it! The point here is that sometimes, hopefully not often, one of your customers is going to be angry about something. The way you handle this situation, and the way you train your employees for encounters like these, is one of those critical areas where you earn the title *manager.*

When a customer is upset, always assume that the situation can go from a spark to a forest fire, and act accordingly. We human beings like to be right. If you tell me that I did something wrong, my first inclination is to prove to you that I did not, or to rationalize the problem by explaining that my apparent wrongness was really right. When we lapse into this basic survival instinct, we become our inner child; in other words, we act like five-year-olds. One could argue that a key to successful adulthood is getting this tendency under control. Assuming that your customers are human beings, I shall therefore assume that they, too, like to be right. So, consider the situation in which your irate customer is convinced that he or she is right and your natural inclination is to also be right. You need to fight this natural inclination. Your only hope for a successful outcome is to stop yourself short, shift away from your basic instinct to defend yourself, and be an adult. Let's break down the "irate customer event" into its basic components:

The customer needs to win, and you need to figure out how. The fundamental rule of negotiating is this: the outcome needs to be a win-win. Only a fool of a negotiator assumes he must drive a bargain where only he comes out on top. Your mind-set, when dealing with the angry customer, has to be, "How can I make this situation a winner for this person?" You may be asking yourself, "But how is this a win-win if I'm only supposed to be concerned about *the other person* winning?" The answer is simple: *you* win by keeping a customer *relationship,* and probably even enhancing it. That's where the win-win comes in.

A battle you cannot win. If there is one thing you need to drill into your employees, as well as yourself, it is this: when a customer wants to argue, you might be able to win the argument with facts and logic, but you lose in the long run because that customer has likely become a non-customer at best, or a "dark legend spreader" at worst. Consider the samurai warrior. Samurai were famously courageous in battle because they *assumed* they were going to die. When dealing with the angry customer, assume you are going to lose the argument and win the battle of keeping a customer.

You must be calm. Understand that your angry customer is busy expressing his inner five- year-old. If you let out your five-year-old to argue with his 5-year old, you have completely blown it, and you might as well arrange for a sit-down meeting in a sandbox. It is not easy to be calm in the face of anger. The way to do it is to *focus completely* on his or her problem. The customer is angry for a reason, whether real or imagined, appropriate or not, and your job is to root out the problem and look for the solution.

Use emotional judo. In the martial art of judo or jiu-jitsu, one uses the weight, force, and strength of an opponent against him. That's how a little gal, skilled in judo, can fling a big guy across a room. Now this analogy can go only so far: I'm not suggesting you start throwing customers around the room. But it is close enough to the real-life way that you can confront a charging opponent without a direct clash. When I ran my legal publishing and research business, we had emotional judo down to an art form. We *had* to. There is nothing like dealing with a pissed-off lawyer to ruin your day. Here is exactly what I would do and what I trained my employees to do. You may want to copy this and paste it to your desk for future reference—it works. Occasionally, I would get a call from my research department that an angry lawyer was on the phone. "Russ, there's a Mr. Smith on line one, and he's really upset about the research we did for him yesterday."

"What's his first name?" I would always ask. (This is crucial. It's much easier to deal with Joe Angry than Mr. Angry.) I would then use a simple ideation technique: I would envision the caller to be a really close friend for whom I would do anything. In reality, he might be the most miserable bastard on the planet, but my mental ideation controls my voice when I pick up the phone. After asking the research assistant for a very brief summary of what he was angry about, I would invariably pick up the phone and say the following: "Hi Joe, this is Russ. Did we screw something up?" Now get the picture here. Joe Smith, Esq. has a bone to pick. As any good trial lawyer would do, he assembled all his facts in logical order, prepared his argument, and was ready to do battle with his opponent (us). Instead, what does he get? My friendly voice and an **attitude** showing that I was basically rolling over and playing dead. And his response was typical: "Oh, I wouldn't say you screwed up. Maybe I wasn't very clear when I placed my request." Now here is a guy who wanted to kill us a few minutes before and is now telling me that maybe it was his fault. After determining what we needed to do to send him the correct research, he asked if we could ship it overnight. "Of course we will," says Mr. Pussycat (me). "But we'll pick up the shipping charges, and you won't be charged for the first search." By the time we get off the phone, Joe Angry has become Joe Buddy. Truth is, in this actual case, the mistake was *entirely* his fault. I discussed the matter with my research director, and she showed me the original fax request in which his assistant asked for exactly what he got. So, I paid for the time of my employees to perform the search, waived the receivable, and even picked up the overnight charges to replace it. So what! I didn't care about the $300 "sale" that was lost. But I did care about the $30,000 per year relationship with that lawyer's firm, and I didn't want him saying anything but good things about us.

Chapter 3 Summary

In this chapter I discussed the following:

- The difference between a sale and a relationship and how worrying about one sale could result in losing hundreds or thousands of future sales.
- Legendary customer service, which is the kind of service that enlists customers to become non-commissioned salespeople for your business.
- Bad Practices are business ideas that are so bad, it seems like somebody dreams them up.
- Bad practice number one is hiring an inexperienced, incompetent receptionist with a goal of saving money.
- What to look for in a good receptionist.
- The telephone and how to use it.
- The irate customer and guidelines for damage control.

CHAPTER 4

Planning

APT Principles: Attitude and Practices

Recall what I said at the beginning of this book: "Those who fail to plan, plan to fail." Planning is far more than just putting down some pro-forma numbers in a spreadsheet. It is more than just hoping to gross five million within the next five years. Planning is at the very core of any successful business. Without a plan, you might achieve some success, but if you are lucky enough not to fail, whatever success you realize will be far less than if you had planned it.

The most difficult feat in planning is military planning. German Field Marshal Helmuth von Moltke is credited with the famous phrase, "No battle plan survives the first contact with the enemy." But his words were not meant to discourage military planning, only to put it in a realistic context. The reason war planning is so difficult is not that your competition (the enemy) is trying to steal market share from you; rather, he is trying to kill you. Battle is chaos, but that doesn't mean that there should be no plan. Imagine D-Day, perhaps the most carefully planned military operation in history. General Eisenhower, a gifted administrator, had his staff draw plans about enemy troop strength, weather conditions, available equipment, topography, civilian population placement, and countless other considerations. We are all too familiar with the history of what happened when the invasion was launched. Shells and bombs missed their targets, gliders overshot their landing zones, landing craft hit the wrong beaches, and somebody didn't notice on the aerial surveillance that the field of battle was covered with huge hedgerows, caused many of the gliders to crash, and which were impossible for tanks to maneuver around. All of the careful plans seemed to go up in smoke, literally. But without the planning, there would have been no way to determine if progress was being made and how slow or fast the objectives were being accomplished. After the chaos of the day, the planning began to pay off. But the real reason the invasion was a success was not the battle plan, but the valor and ingenuity of the men who fought the battle. Notice that I say ingenuity immediately after valor. American officers and non-coms were trained to expect the unexpected and were relied on to make decisions on the spot. Through the smoke and bloodshed, it may have seemed like the plan had gone awry, but that was not the case. Flexibility and swift reaction to changing battle realities were *part of the plan itself.* Compare this to the hide-bound stiffness of the German command structure. The reality on the ground—the Normandy Invasion—did not change the mind of the German high command, who believed that the invasion would come not at Normandy, but at Calais, about 86 miles away. Because the officers at heavily fortified Calais could not make their decisions based on reports from Normandy, they did not rush their heavy tanks to the battle because that would have been a change in plan—and changes in the plan had to come from Berlin. It's bad planning not to plan for flexibility.

There are many reasons, all bad, why people fail to plan. As I go through the reasons below, ask yourself if they apply to you.

"There are too many variables over which I have no control, so careful planning is unrealistic." Yes, there are variables, countless ones at that. Let's examine just a few variables over which you really have no control: the economy, interest rates, political realities, war, climate, crime, vandalism, terrorism, employee illness, government regulations, changes in market preferences, competition, and so on. This list could go on for pages. The big question you need to ask yourself is, "So what?" Variables in business, just as in life, will always be there. Of course you can't control them, but you can ensure that they don't control you. You should look at the variables in life as you look at the weather: it's good, it's bad, and it changes. With a solid plan, you can manage the variables. If you don't plan, you are under the total dominance of the variables. Recall the discussion of D-Day above. Imagine if Eisenhower's staff members threw up their hands and declared that the invasion could not be planned for because there were too many variables. The world map might look very different.

"It's too difficult." Nothing important in life is worthwhile unless there is some struggle to achieve it. Planning is simply a project that consists of many parts. Once broken down into manageable pieces, the process itself becomes a lot easier. How do you build a cathedral? One brick at a time. But here is where **attitude** comes significantly into play. If you hold planning in your mind as a difficult process, you guarantee its difficulty! Consider the possibility that planning is fun. Planning is where you put your dreams down on paper, where you let your thoughts soar and allow your imagination to run wild (well, not too wild). Planning is the process in which you grab that great idea and start to build a structure to give it form. *Attitude!*

The goal-setting part of a business plan gives a lot of people heartburn. "I get hung up on goal-setting because it's just words or numbers on paper." I have spoken to many entrepreneurs who have expressed this concern, and the issue always seems to come down to a gut-level lack of belief in the planning process itself. I will examine this phenomenon in detail later in this chapter, but for now just understand this: once you begin the process, you need to allow yourself to be swept along with it. Once planning begins, those words and numbers on the paper start to look *very real*.

"I have planned in the past, but I never seem to stick with it." The key here is very simple. A plan ignored is worse than no plan at all because you will have wasted the time spent on the plan in the first place, time that you could have spent bouncing aimlessly off walls, which is exactly what you will be doing if you have ignored the plan. Back to D-Day. One of my favorite parts of the movie *The Longest Day* was the scene where General Theodore Roosevelt, TR's son, played by Henry Fonda, found himself and his unit in the right country—but on the wrong beach. He could have said, "The plan is screwed. We may as well hitch a ride back to the ship." But he didn't. Instead he said, "Well, it looks like the war starts right here." From there he continued to execute the plan, although from a different location. Any plan must be constantly read, referred to, clipped and pasted in various places, and amended as needed. Think of your plan *not* as a document, but as a guidebook or map. Parts of your plan should be in your calendar book or PDA, or even taped to your mirror. As always, use the *APT Principle* to keep you focused.

"Every time I begin a plan, I get sidetracked." Planning can be a lonely process, but it shouldn't be. It's easy to postpone an effort for another day when the only person you have to answer to is yourself. I strongly encourage you to enlist the aid of someone else, preferably a group of people, to help you work through the process. This may be your spouse, business partner, fellow executives, or a professional business coach. A business coach is a paid consultant who works with you to help you achieve the potential of your business. I discuss the profession of business coaching in Chapter 13. The worst time to plan is when you *feel like it*. This can be the death of a plan before it even comes to life. Planning activities should be recorded on your calendar and looked at with the seriousness of your spouse's birthday or your anniversary.

Goal Setting

Goals drive people sane. I heard that in a seminar some years ago, and its truth still resonates with me. Think of a time when you had nothing to do. If you're very busy, the concept might seem enticing, but recall your physical and mental state during that time of emptiness. There was nothing driving you, just time to *relax*. At the beginning of this period, whether it was a vacation or just a long weekend, the prospect of having nothing to strive for looked pretty good. No deadline, no plan checking, no to-do list—just a wide open space of time. If you're honest with yourself, you will admit that you experienced uneasiness. This happened to me after I sold my company. The day the post-acquisition consulting engagement ended, I felt great. I was financially independent and had no more of the daily grind of business. Free from the daily pressure, free to do what I pleased, free to relax, free to have fun! That lasted about a week. Without having goals to shoot for, my days were dominated by handling trivial matters. What was once a simple task suddenly became a half-day project. All of those things that I would delegate to my staff were now mine to handle because I had no more staff. Now, I'm not saying that your goals, including retirement goals, should always be business oriented. Improving you golf game, learning to paint, or taking up sailboat racing are all fine goals...but they *are* goals. Nor am I saying that you shouldn't have a completely relaxing vacation or long weekend. Just observe that drifting creates no sense of accomplishment, no sense of worth, no pleasure. Setting and achieving a goal, even if your goal is to read a long-neglected novel, creates more pleasure than just waiting for something to show up.

Author Leo B. Helzel wrote a book with a wonderful title: *A Goal is a Dream with a Deadline* (McGraw-Hill, 1995). There is beauty in that phrase, and truth. We all dream of what the future should look like. Unless those dreams are broken down and converted into goals, when the future becomes the present, you will have nothing but your dreams. That is a nightmare! As George Will so aptly put it, "The future has a way of arriving unannounced."

The SMART Principle of Goal Setting

I don't know who came up with the SMART acronym for goal setting, but he or she was brilliant. It forms a basis for any step toward setting goals and should be adhered to. Here is what the SMART principle holds. A goal should be the following:

Specific: Define your goal in exact language. This is where you turn a dream into a goal, as will be discussed shortly. This is the mental space that you begin to populate with the tangible stuff. "I will open a new branch within 10 miles" beats "I will expand."

Measurable: Set forth your goals and their intermediate benchmarks in a way that can be actually measured, both at the end and at every step of the way. The measurement could be dollars, mailing pieces sent, appointments, sales closed, or new clients signed up. Most organizations involved in direct sales have statistics breaking down each part of the sales process. For example, the statistics may show that for every 50 calls you make, you will get three appointments. For every three appointments, the statistics show that you will close one sale. The average commission on a closed sale is $1,200. Therefore, every call is worth $24 ($1,200 divided by 50)—just for making the call. Want $24? Pick up the phone.

Achievable: Is it possible to reach your goal within the set period, given the resources that you will need? Don't hope that something will show up; make sure you have the resources, or at least access to the resources to make the goal achievable. "I will renovate 100 new kitchens within six months." Well, that's very exciting, but you'd better have a contact list filled with subcontractors who have nothing else to do in the next half year. An unachievable goal will only lead to frustration; THAT will turn you off on the whole goal-setting process.

Realistic: Is your goal based on reality, or is it a fantasy? An unrealistic goal is unlikely to be met and can only lead to your disappointment. If it's realistic, you can form a mental picture of your goal. Once you have that mental picture, a picture you can really be a part of, your goal will have a real life. A week after opening your doors, I don't suggest that your goal setting include "I will be bigger than Microsoft within a year."

Timed: It is crucial to place a time limit for achieving a goal; otherwise, it remains a dream. Timed goals lend themselves to charts, especially bar charts. Think of hospital fundraising campaigns, which are often accompanied by a big bar chart right by the entrance. Every week or month, or whatever period is appropriate, you can gauge the progress. This is one of the fun parts of business. I love working with Excel. I mastered it enough to know how to do all kinds of charts based on the underlying numbers. Many people think of a spreadsheet as a tool for showing them what has happened. Open your mind to it as a tool for charting the future—for goal setting. If you don't know how to use Excel, you should consider taking a course. It will be worth your time and money.

Most business writers and consultants, myself included, would add one other element to the list: your goal should be CHALLENGING. It may not fit nicely into the acronym, but it is essential. Suppose, for example, you are a real estate broker, and you sell an average of two houses per month at an average price of $250,000 ($6 million gross sales per year), and you set forth a goal of increasing your house sales by three per year. This is obviously *S*pecific, *M*easurable, *A*chievable, *R*ealistic, and *T*imed, but so what? There is nothing challenging or exciting about the goal. How about one additional sale per *month*, or twelve per year? This would bring your gross sales up to $9 million. Remember, for goals to be meaningful, they must be dream-based. Realistic, yes, but also exciting. Yes, I know that as I am writing this, we are in a horrible real estate slump. But working through the SMART principle of goal setting and adding the word *challenging*, will get you to your goal faster than by bitching about the market to the folks at the diner. ***Attitude!***

Goals and Dreams Are For Life, Not Just For Business

As you begin your goal-setting adventure, you should organize goals into categories. The number of categories is limited only by your own imagination, but I suggest that you start with just a few. Here are my recommendations in alphabetical order:

Business Goals
Family Goals
Financial Goals (personal)
Fun Goals
Charitable Goals

Turning Dreams into Goals

Dreams are great. Without them you are really not in the game of living up to your potential. But dreams are fuzzy; they have no sharp edges and can meander into mental mush. Remember Helzel's book, *A Goal is a Dream with a Deadline?* Try the following exercise, which is closely tied to the Specific part of the SMART principle. On the left-hand side of a piece of paper, list your dreams, broken down by category. On the right-hand side, turn that dream into a goal by making it Specific.

Business Goals

Dream: To build a successful business. **Goal:** To achieve $5 million in revenues and $1 million in net profits by December 2014.

Dream: To own my own office building someday. **Goal:** I will purchase a four thousand-square-foot building within 10 miles by July 2013.

Family Goals

Dream: To spend more vacation time with my family. **Goal**: To purchase a vacation house within 100 miles in the next 12 months.

Dream: To have family projects that we can all enjoy. **Goal**: With my family's input, I will come up with a list of 12 monthly projects by February 2012.

Financial Goals

Dream: To build a retirement nest egg. **Goal**: To accumulate $3 million in liquid assets by age 65 (break this down to monthly or at least annual amounts).

Dream: To be debt free. **Goal**: Meet with my financial planner and develop a plan to be debt free within 10 years.

Fun Goals

Dream: To be a really good golfer. **Goal:** To knock 10 points off my game in the next year by practicing daily for one hour and taking monthly refresher lessons.

Dream: To learn to enjoy fishing. **Goal:** I will research and decide on an instructor or group that will teach me how to fish by November 1 of this year.

Charitable Goals

Dream: To give more to charity. **Goal:** I will donate $5,000 to my five favorite charities by 2013.

Dream: I would like to help combat illiteracy. **Goal**: I will contact local literacy groups and become a literacy volunteer within 60 days from now.

Goal setting is fun. You might have 10 or more dreams for each of the above categories. How about setting a goal RIGHT NOW? When will you schedule your first dream-to-goal conversion session?

The Formal Business Plan

Should you have a formal business plan? YES. I hate to be so blunt and to burden you with a complicated task, but you really need to take the time to write a formal business plan. Here's why: it puts the smarts into the SMART principle of goal setting. All of the elements of SMART are contained in a well-executed business plan: Specific, Measurable, Achievable, Realistic, and Timed. And, don't forget the part that doesn't fit into the acronym: "C" for Challenging.

A business plan is a "how-to book" specifically designed for your business. Think of it as a manual for how to get it done, the "it" being the sum of your goals. When you buy a new car, you get a huge owner's manual and login instructions to a website with a gazillion megabytes. Doesn't your business deserve as much?

The business plan is written on paper, not carved in stone, and it should be amended to account for new opportunities and realities. It is not a constitution and need not go through a complicated process for amendment. We often hear the famous quote "Make a decision and stick to it." I don't know who said that, but I question its wisdom. By all means stick to a decision, including all of those decisions in a business plan, BUT, be willing to change your decision and your plans when reality, including new opportunities, dictates. In Barbara Tuchman's book *The Guns of August*, she discussed how World War I could have been avoided, if only the German general staff been willing to reverse the decision to mobilize for war. Nothing in a plan, military or business, should be considered carved into granite.

The business plan focuses you like no other document in your office. It should be referred to regularly and with discipline. Make an appointment in your calendar to review it monthly.

Finally—and this is by no means least in importance— you may need the business plan to raise capital, whether by bank financing or equity investment. I remember the hair dresser character played by Warren Beatty in the movie *Shampoo.* In a great scene he is sitting with a banker, trying to convince Mr. Green Eyeshades to make a loan so that he could set up his own salon. As the banker is trying to get Beatty to give him specific reasons why he should make the loan, all the hapless, would-be entrepreneur can say is, "I got the heads" (meaning his lady followers). Not exactly a formal business plan.

Don't Make it Complicated (Any More Than Necessary)

I am convinced that a lot of business people are intimidated by the complexity of the many business planning software tools out there. This is not the fault of the business plan software developers, bless their hearts, because they only mean to give you everything that you could possibly need. But many of the modules in the various programs do not apply to the basic small business. If your business is one you have no intentions of going public, or one for which you have no thoughts of seeking equity financing, you should err on the side of making the plan simple—or else you will never get it done! If you do plan major financing, whether debt or equity, you will want some consulting horsepower under your hood anyway. There are professionals who can assist you in writing the complex plan. There is also software to make the task easier. I have used Business Plan Pro, by PaloAlto Software and have found it to be quite good. See www. businessplanpro.com. They'll take you through the plan, step by step, and provide an explanation and examples for each module of the plan.

Components of the Formal Business Plan

Executive summary: This is a top-level overview of your business, essential for any third party, such as a banker. You do not want to bore a banker. They are boring enough. Use this to explain what your business is, what you're up to, and why the reader of your plan may want to lend or invest.

Objectives: This part is important if financing is one of the purposes of the plan. It is also a useful guide for you, and it should be written with your goals right next to you. Items such as "break even by 2014" or "sales of $5 million or net profit of $1 million by 2015" should be listed here.

Mission: A mission statement isn't just for companies like IBM; it allows you to express your vision for your business. You need to spend some time on this and turn your thoughts loose. It should be inspirational, thought provoking, and realistic. Part of Google's mission statement is "Don't be Evil." I always found this to be weird. Don't we all want to avoid evil without necessarily stating it? When writing your mission statement you might want to be guided by a principle: "don't write stupid sounding mission statements." Once your mission statement is written, you should memorize it and post it prominently throughout your office.

Keys to success: List, as extensively as possible, the major components that you see as the keys that will unlock your goals. It may include providing regular sales training, developing community relationships, hiring a skilled IT professional, or marketing through direct mail campaigns. You are the expert here. This is a good place to focus your thoughts. Here you develop Best Practices.

Company summary: This is a thumbnail of your business, not as detailed as the executive summary. This is one of the many useful places for a third party to quickly refer.

Company ownership: This is a brief statement that describes who owns your business, whether shareholders in a corporation, partners in a partnership, or members in a limited liability company (LLC).

Start-up summary: If this applies to you, it is a summary of the steps it will take to start the business, including a synopsis of the costs from the next section. It should be compelling and realistic. If someone—you for that matter—sees a huge revenue projection for the first year with only minor costs, you are kidding nobody but yourself.

Start-up costs: Again, if this applies to you, make it detailed and realistic. Be specific in coming up with your numbers. If your initial costs involve heavy direct mail advertising, check to see if a postal rate increase is on the horizon, and don't forget the cost of the envelopes and return postage.

Company location and physical facilities: Be detailed. If there is something good to say, such as "excellent high-profile location," say it here and include photographs.

Services: A summary of everything that your company provides.

Services (detailed description): This is a good place to focus on all the services you provide, including some that may surprise you. A friend of mine had a large graphic design company that also served as a free drop-off point for advertising agencies to submit entries for advertising award competitions. This brought in no revenue, but it was a powerful public relations tool and rainmaker for his design business.

Competition: Nobody wants to think about it, but this is where you must think about it—carefully. This is an opportunity to distinguish yourself from the competition without trying to pull the wool over your own eyes. I have a young friend who asked me recently to kick around an idea he had for an Internet business. His concept was to provide a site for people to give their opinions of local tradespeople and other businesses and professionals. I asked him if he ever heard of Angie's List, the 12 foot gorilla of consumer sentiment sites. He never heard of it. If someone has "occupied the space" (to use a phrase from the Internet), you should face head-on how you will muscle into that space. I'm not saying that you should not proceed in the face of competition—far from it. Just be aware of who your competitors are and how you can be better.

Sales literature: Provide a brief description of your current literature, and insert copies of the brochures on the following pages or in an appendix. This is a good place to refer to your website for updates—and another reason to make sure your website is just that: up-to-date.

Fulfillment: Think of fulfillment as how you provide your service or product, if applicable. Depending on what you are selling, fulfillment costs can be quite high, but it can also be an area for improved profitability. Some companies find that they can improve the bottom line by purchasing UPS or Federal Express labels in bulk and charging the customer a reasonable shipping and handling fee.

Future services: Allow your marketing mind to go wild, and think about additional services you may bring to market. An insurance broker, for example, may think about providing fee-based risk management services. I know a food distributor who has an extensive list of training courses for the food industry. He has turned himself into the regional food university. He charges for the courses and, more important, converts a lot of the attendees into customers.

Market analysis: What and who is the market for your goods and services? Spend some time here; you may come up with markets that you never thought of. I know an ambitious young woman who opened an organic fresh foods deli. The reason she didn't have a lot of competition is that selling fresh organic foods is very expensive, but she saw markets where a lesser mortal may have only seen high food costs. She supplies lunch services to large corporations and university meetings—people who love to feel that they are helping the environment and can afford her necessarily high prices. Can you see how the business plan is not just a place to write things but an actual tool for helping you create your business?

Market segmentation: Using the insurance broker example again, she may have thought her market was homeowners but, upon examination, realized that 60 percent came from businesses with a minimum of 20 employees. The first place to look is your market as it exists now, unless of course you are a start-up. By looking at what you have and then imagining where you can go, you will come up with ideas about how you can target certain market segments. I have a dentist friend who realized that a large part of his new practice might be children. He hooked up a VCR (this was a few years ago – today it would be a DVD player) in the waiting room and showed child-oriented dental health videos. The parents loved it, and they spread the word.

Market segment strategy: If you have identified segmentation, what is your plan to capitalize on that knowledge? Just as my dentist friend above, you can come up with all sorts of imaginative ways to strategize on market segmentation. I know a guy who immigrated to the United States from Brazil many years ago. He realized that Portuguese is not a commonly spoken language in America, especially Brazilian Portuguese. He has a successful limousine and tour business, catering strictly to Brazilian tourists and business people.

Market needs: What is your market missing? Come up with the answers to that question and combine it with your ability to provide it, and your business plan will be a success just from this module. When I began my first publishing venture, *The New York Jury Verdict Reporter,* I realized that the New York legal market was sorely lacking reliable information on civil jury verdicts. Lawyers used to settle cases using the wildest of case evaluation methods, my favorite being "three times special [actual] damages." Nonsense. A case is worth what juries tend to award for certain injuries, and reliable data about what real juries awarded was exactly what my publication provided. The market loved it and paid me handsomely for it.

Market trends: Here you will need to do some research. You should not answer this question from your "gut feeling," although the feeling in your gut often leads you to some very interesting research. Some people might say that the way to spot market trends is simply to study what the late, great Steve Jobs did. But Steve Jobs was a rare force of nature—he didn't spot trends, he made them. Read the business pages of newspapers, subscribe to good business magazines, like *Forbes,* and attend trade shows. Keep in motion, and keep your eyes and ears open.

Market growth: You will learn about market growth during your research on market trends. If you are in a very slow growing market or a stagnant one, you have some serious analysis ahead of you. When was the last time you saw a TV repair shop? A long time ago. Once, this was a thriving industry, but with the advent of printed circuit boards replacing vacuum tubes, the TV repair market and TV repair shops disappeared almost overnight. Look at some of the other things that were once all the rage and are now disappearing: fax machines (replaced with e-mail attachments or virtual fax services) and CD-ROMs, which were extremely popular a few years ago, just around the time that the Internet came into its own. We were amazed at the massive storage capacity of a typical CD-ROM: 650 megabytes. Now, a $15 flash drive can hold many gigabytes. If you believe the late Steve Jobs (and who doesn't believe Steve Jobs), our storage needs in the future will be in "the Cloud," not on a physical device.

Your business analysis: Here you'll discuss *your* specific business, its prospects, and how it fits into the marketplace. It should be a clearly written narrative, explaining everything about the market and your business that you can think of. People often make the mistake of writing befuddling jargon or stilted words. Clear writing is for everyone, including you when you refer back to your plan in the future. Would you rather read "We work within a demographic paradigm of differential age cohorts" or "Our market is spread over different age groups"?

Sales forecast: This will be presented in graphs, charts, or diagrams, accompanied by a text summary. Recall that very funny TV commercial for Federal Express where an assistant security checker calls his boss to look at the air traveler's bound portfolio. "He's leading with sales figures," yells the assistant, while the security supervisor says, "I'm bored" and then starts to snore. There is a lesson to be learned here: save the good stuff, including sales projections, for later to build a sense of suspense—assuming your plan is aimed at a potential financier—and, by all means, use color. Did I mention, don't exaggerate—and watch your credibility?

Strategic alliances: If you have them, this is the place to discuss them. Traditional shippers hook up with Internet powerhouses, grocers align with food distributers, and software developers pal around with business seminar groups. A strategic alliance can move your business forward much further than its own resources alone. A strategic alliance is a classic win-win for all members of the alliance.

Milestones: What are the major milestones that you want to achieve? Some examples might include logo design, a commercial website, or a computer network setup. These milestones should be specific and should include budget numbers and estimated dates of completion. Some milestones must be reached before other things can happen. For example, you would not want to do a direct mail campaign before you have a well-functioning website to which you will refer in the direct mail pieces. "Coming soon" often means "We don't have a lot of capital, so we're trying to bootstrap it." Don't call attention to problems, and that's why planning your milestones carefully is critical.

Management summary: This is a discussion of your management team, or yourself, if you *are* the team at present. Say as many good things about your key people as possible. If Melissa Jones, your finance manager, graduated from SUNY at Oneonta, that's fine, but don't leave out the fact that she graduated *magna cum laude* and won the finance medal.

Management team gaps: You need to carefully analyze what is missing from your team. Some personnel positions, such as IT, can be farmed out; but others, such as finance and accounting, might need to be in place as hired managers. Here, you should also include a discussion of future plans for hiring managers.

Financial plan: Do you intend to finance future growth through cash flow, debt, or equity financing? You'll want to include a textual review here accompanied by financials. The plan should show a projected income statement, cash flow forecast, and balance sheet. It might be helpful to break these out as separate main headings.

Assumptions: Any future-looking financial plan is based on assumptions. You assume that you will sell X number of widgets or have X number of clients/customers paying you Y amount of dollars while you spend Z amount in expenses. These assumptions should all be in your plan. If you are working in an Excel spreadsheet, these assumptions should appear at the bottom or as comments in a data cell (comments are the little text bubbles that appears when you hover your mouse over the cell). Did you ever look at a financial statement entry and ask yourself, "What the hell does this mean?" In a business plan, you, or anyone reading it, should never have to ask that question.

Breakeven analysis: This important part of your financial plan shows, based on your assumptions, how much business you need to break even at a point in the future. If yours is an existing business, this may not be appropriate, unless you haven't broken even yet. But in the hands of a competent spreadsheet designer, it can be exciting to show that you broke even two years ago and are now on a serious profit trajectory. If you are a start-up, knowing when you can expect to break even is a question of major importance. How much cash, your own or a bank's or investor's, will you "burn through" before the red ink turns black?

Ratios: You should discuss business ratios with your accountant, who should point you to resources for finding key ratios for your type of business or industry. This is something that any accountant should do as a matter of course, in my opinion, but it is not always done. Ask for it. If he doesn't provide it, ask for it louder. Reading ratios is a good skill to develop. A seasoned financial person can breeze through a complex set of financials in short order because he or she knows what ratios to look for, since they are key indicators of the health of a business.

A Note for Not-for-Profits

As I said earlier, a business plan is not just a process for profit-making enterprises. Most of what goes into a business plan for a profit-seeking enterprise is identical to what a not-for-profit organization should have in its plan. The purpose of the business plan is the same for each type of organization, including plans for getting money. You write a typical business plan with a view that a banker or investor might someday look at it. In a not-for-profit, grant-giving foundations and government agencies replace bankers and investors. Just as with any-one from whom you are seeking funding, they want to see a business plan. PaloAlto Software, the company that created Business Plan Pro, has sample plans for not-for-profit organizations. If you are a non-for-profit organization, you must have a business plan, if for no other reason than applying for grants.

Chapter 4 Summary

In this chapter I discussed the following:

- An overview of planning and why people don't plan
- Goal setting: A goal is a dream with a deadline
- The SMART principle of goal setting
- Goals are for life, not just for business
- Turning dreams into goals
- The formal business plan
- Business plan software
- Plans for not-for-profit organizations in order to get grants

CHAPTER 5

Go it Alone or Partner?

APT Principle: Attitude

If you are starting a business, or own an existing one, a major question is whether you want to be the sole owner or partner with someone. Just to be clear, when I talk about sole owner, I include in that phrase married couples and members of your immediate family. When I say partner, I mean a non-family member who owns part of your business, including shareholders of corporations and members of a limited liability company (LLC). In other words, a *partner,* as I use the word in this chapter, is not limited to a legal partnership, but to the other forms of doing business as well. You always hear lawyers and accountants, whose practice may be a corporation or LLC, referring to their co-owners as "partners."

Quick Primer on the Different Ways of Doing Business

You can find countless sources of information about the different ways of doing business, but the most important sources are your lawyer and accountant. What follows is a brief overview of the legal forms for doing business. Don't make a decision based on what follows: talk to your advisors.

Sole proprietorship: This is the simplest way to do business. After the necessary organizational details (stationery, location, phone, etc.), you start doing business. You will need an assumed name certificate, also known as a "DBA" (Doing Business As) from your local government. You *are* the business and the business *is* you. If the business screws something up, it's you who are solely responsible. In other words, Harry's Diner is not liable, Harry is. There is no separate tax return to file, but of course you have to carefully document your deductible expenses. You don't have to pay annual state corporation taxes, and you save on accounting fees. When you die or become disabled, the business dies or becomes disabled as well. It's a simple way of doing business. It's also simply bad. The lack of continuity, the legal exposure, and the inability to raise equity capital all makes this form of doing business not worth the dollars saved, unless your business idea is a very small one.

Partnership: A partnership is two or more people doing business together. But this is an oversimplification because every state has a detailed partnership law. Keep in mind that for tax purposes, all profits and losses flow through to the partners; when one partner leaves or dies, the partnership ends and a new one must be formed. Moreover, all of the partners are equally responsible for the actions of the other partners. On this last point, you may ask, "Does this mean that if my partner incurs a five million-dollar judgment, I can be liable?" Yes, that's exactly what it means. This is why, although insurance can protect against a lot of things, the partnership method of doing business is becoming less and less popular. It can be an exciting way of doing business, as well as an exciting way of getting your financial ass handed to you if one of your trusted partners screws up big time. Imagine if you were Bernie Madoff's partner?

Corporation: In the corporate way of doing business, you and your co-owners own shares of stock in the corporation. A separate tax return, both state and federal, must be filed, and books must be carefully kept. There are annual filing fees and, depending on the type of corporation, separate taxes on corporate earnings. The typical corporation is known as a "C" corporation, and it pays taxes in addition to the taxes that the shareholders pay.

S corporation: An "S" corporation, formerly known as and still often referred to as a "Subchapter S corporation," is an IRS code exception that allows for profits and losses to flow directly through to shareholders without the corporation paying separate taxes, similar to a partnership. There is a rule of thumb one often hears, which states that if the corporation is making money, it should be a C corporation because the corporate tax rate is lower; if it's losing money, on the other hand, it should be an S corporation because the shareholder(s) can write off the losses on their individual returns. Like many old sayings, it is only partially trustworthy since there are other reasons why you might want to be an S corporation. When you sell your corporation, there are huge tax advantages to being an S corporation. An S corporation is also more attractive to a buyer because the buyer acquires the *assets* of your S corporation, not its stock. This means that the acquirer does not assume your liabilities unless specifically agreed to. When trying to sell a business, many small business owners rue the day they incorporated without electing S status.

Limited Liability Company (LLC): This is becoming the most popular way of doing business because it combines the limited liability and continuity of a corporation with the tax advantages of a partnership. There is more flexibility with profit and loss pass-through than with an S corporation. Formation is a bit more complicated because you are required to advertise the name prior to formation, rather than simply clearing it through your state's Secretary of State. Owners are called "members" rather than shareholders. Many people have a hard time getting this, although I don't know why. A few years ago I refinanced a commercial property I owned that was an LLC. I received countless calls from the closing department at the bank asking who the *president* of the corporation was. It was not a corporation, but an LLC, I explained, and I was the "managing member," not the president. Well, apparently the bank forms had a place for the president's signature, but no place for a managing member. I finally surrendered to the bureaucracy and said, "Fine, I'm the president." Again, discuss this with your tax and legal advisors. Caution: although most lawyers are familiar with the LLC as a way of doing business, many are stuck in the old, familiar ways of forming a corporation. A lot of businesses are incorporated, rather than formed as an LLC, simply because the lawyer didn't know what to do with an LLC. An LLC might be the best option for you; make sure your lawyer is on top of the game.

Benefits of Sole Ownership

Any business writer, when listing the benefits of some-thing, always lists those things that the writer *perceives* as benefits. You the reader may see a particular point not as a benefit, but as a detriment. A marathon is 26 miles long. That's a big detriment to me, but to a running fanatic, it's a benefit. Just a warning! That said, these are what I consider the benefits of being a sole owner. (By sole owner, I am not advocating the business form of sole proprietorship, but just the idea of operating on your own.) You can, and usually should be, a corporation or an LLC, even if it's only you. So here, in my opinion, are the benefits of going it alone:

No one to answer to: Other than the usual suspects, including your spouse, the IRS, your banker, your ven-dors and, of course, your customers.

Flexible business planning: When you come up with a new idea, you do not have to sell it to partners; you can just charge ahead. Remember—I said that these are ben-efits *as perceived by me.* Many a sole owner has charged ahead into a brick wall, unaware of the wall because there was no partner to point it out. But even if you are not the impetuous type and are careful about taking leaps, being on your own means not agonizing over how to convince a partner that your idea is sound.

Pride of ownership: "*I* built this," not "*We* built this." You don't have to share the glory. Many (most?)

entrepreneurs are in business for the thrill and joy of making big things happen.

Simplicity of decision making: No committees! It's your call. Sometimes another person can help you simplify things, but that other person does not have to be a business partner. It could be a confidant with whom you meet regularly to share ideas, a friend or, of course, your spouse. It could be a consultant or a business coach, about which more will be discussed in Chapter 13.

Nothing to disentangle: Splitting a business relationship is often unpleasant, even with carefully crafted business agreements. A business split means an unbundling of years of plans and actions. It is also expensive, and it chews up vast hours of the accountant's and lawyer's time. It can also take an emotional toll. People usually don't end relationships because everything is going well.

Ease of sale: Is it time to cash out? Just put your business up for sale. You decide what is a good deal after you consult with your advisors. Many a sale has come to a screeching halt because the partners could not agree on the terms of the buyout.

Emotional issues: With all of the challenges of business, at least you don't have to worry about disagreements with partners. If you have endless problems with an employee, you can simply show him the door. With a partner, you live the life of a negotiator.

Benefits of Shared Ownership

All of you dyed-in-wool loners out there will probably ignore the following benefits of having a partner. But don't say I didn't tell you, because there *are* benefits.

Plugs management talent gaps: A good partnership brings multiple talents to the game. One partner may lack financial skills, while the other partner is an expert; one partner might hate sales, while the other enjoys it and is good at it. One partner can be shy and the other the life of the party. Different personality types can not only work well together, but can actually work better than two people who are the same type. An aggressive Type A personality might make a good entrepreneur but could be a lousy partner for another Type A.

Expanded business contacts: Each partner brings his or her own circle of contacts to the business, theoretically expanding the business by that other person's presence. Networking is one of the best ways to grow any business—an essential part of marketing. With a partner, your networking opportunities expand. You join Rotary; your partner joins the Lions Club.

Easier capital access: If you have roughly equal talents, a capital source will be more convinced of the future continuity of a business. A banker or an investor might be impressed with the owner of the business but will have a natural concern about the health of the business should the health of the business owner fail.

Shared responsibilities: When you go on vacation, it's nice to know there is someone there with a vested interest in making things work. A loyal, well-trained employee can fit the bill, but there is nothing like having skin in the game to focus your attention. When I owned my company, I had no partner other than my wonderful wife. Once, while we were relaxing in the Caribbean, we heard about a blizzard on Long Island. We didn't worry because our trusted office manager was in charge. When we returned, we found out that she had simply closed the office for two days, rather than arrange for late starts or staggering shifts, as any owner would do. There's nothing like a vested interest.

Pride of ownership: No, this is not a typo. Although this item also appears under the benefits of sole ownership, with a partner you can take comfort that when you go, the business doesn't go with you. There is a built-in continuity. Note: See discussion about business agreements below. If you have been fortunate enough to have a partner with whom you are totally compatible, you will actually enjoy seeing your partner's success as well as your own.

High performance teamwork: With the right partner(s), your ability to multiply your efforts and talents expand enormously. Working with a partner can be a fulfilling and profitable experience for both (or all) of you. Think of Abbott without Costello. Multiple talents, contacts, and strengths amplify the entrepreneurial drive that makes a business work.

Shared Ownership Concerns: Legal Issues

It has often been said that choosing a business partner is similar to choosing a spouse. Yes, there are similarities, but also major differences. If you are a traditionalist like me, you believe that choosing a spouse involves making a solemn vow tied to a contract of marriage, that this is your life partner. A business partnership, on the other hand, includes no vow that this person or persons will be with you for life, but it absolutely does—or should—involve a contract. ***APT Alert: Practice*** This is one of those places where I tell you that if you get this point, this book will have paid for itself a thousand fold. When you take on a partner, or a major shareholder, *sign a business agreement.* Obviously, this means that you must hammer out the details *before* you form the business. This is not the place to economize—hire a lawyer. In the long run, it is your best investment. By the way, what is the difference between a contract and an agreement? Nothing. They mean exactly the same thing, and I use them interchangeably.

I was approached a few of years ago by a group of 10 guys, one of whom was a very good friend and still is, who wanted me to invest in a food company they were forming. My investment was to be $50,000 for which I would get 10 percent of the limited liability company (LLC). I looked at their first draft of a business plan, consulted with some people in the industry, and concluded that it looked like a good investment. "Okay, I'm in," I said. "Just send me the Articles of Organization and the Operating Agreement" (the minimum documents for an

LLC). "Well," said my friend, "you have to understand that these guys are used to doing business on a hand shake. They just want to get things operating and worry about the *legalities* later." The next section describes why I chose not to invest.

Why You Need a Business Agreement

Shortly, you'll learn why I turned down that investment, and why you should not consider any multi-owner business arrangement unless the "legalities" have been taken care of in advance.

Everybody is in love at the beginning. (Remember the song "Will You Still Love Me Tomorrow"?) You and your future partners have come up with a great idea and are excited about launching it. The future looks great— what business idea doesn't have a great future? The market looks great, the product line looks great, your partner-to-be looks great and, to him, you look great. Ain't life great?! Any possible disagreement will be smoothed out easily. If something unforeseen happens, you'll handle it then. Why waste time on nit-picking details now? You guys have a business to launch. Well, pardon me for being unromantic, but let me disturb your romantic notions with a few questions. What happens if you or your partner dies or becomes disabled? Just a "legality"? What happens if you reach a point where you are deadlocked over a decision? Just a "legality"? What happens if you or your partner want to sell out his or your interest? Just a "legality"? What happens if one of your family members wants to join the business? Just a "legality"? What happens if one of you wants to go into debt and the other doesn't? Just a "legality"? Do you find these questions troubling? You should. At the typical organizational love fest, well-meaning business people too often dismiss these questions as just "legalities" to be taken care of later. This is just like taking your boat out into the ocean and checking your fuel supply *later.* In the true example I discussed above, none of the legalities were handled up front, and the inevitable occurred. There was constant squabbling about investing in new equipment and inventory versus taking dividends from the start. This is, and can always be, a major stumbling point. None of the investors were kids. Some of them thought that the idea of plowing back money into the business wasn't the way their money should work, and taking out some of the profits just seemed like a good idea. To complicate matters, there was never an understanding about who was to do what. Who was going to be the boss and make important decisions every day without getting an opinion from the rest of the gang? The business totally failed after about two years. I'm glad I passed it up, saving myself $50,000 as well as my pal's continuing friendship. I never tell someone "I told you so" because I believe only a smartass would say that, especially to a friend. But my friend volunteered, "You told us so."

An oral agreement isn't worth the paper it's written on: Legally, not all contracts have to be written. Some contracts must be in writing, such as a contract to sell real estate. The law that requires some contracts to be in writing is known as the statute of frauds, and it dates back to seventeenth-century England. In the

United States, the statute of frauds is part of the Uniform Commercial Code. Contracts that must be in writing to be valid include marriage contracts, real estate contracts, and contracts that cannot be completed within one year. I won't review the entire law here, but this is what you need to know about contracts: if an agreement is *important,* get it in writing, whether or not it is required by the statute of frauds. What is important? Don't bother trying to answer that question: get *every* agreement in writing. After buying a new house, I was approached by a couple of guys who provided swimming pool cleaning and maintenance services. They told me they would open the pool within a couple of weeks of Memorial Day; they would clean it once a week; they would put in chlorine and other chemicals as required; they would clean out the intake traps and keep the lines clear; they also said that they would close the pool within a couple of weeks of Labor Day; and, finally, they would put on the winter cover. The costs might vary, they told me, depending on circumstances like weather and chemical needs. Lots of information, yes? I said that sounds fine; just prepare the contract so I can review it. The chief guy looked at me as if I had just insulted his mother, put out his hand, and said, "Here is my contract." They didn't get the point—or the job. If all of those words can be spoken, they can be written. Compare this to a contractor who did work on our vacation house in Pennsylvania. Every now and then, I would ask him to perform some tasks, such as installing a couple of new electric boxes, repair a portion of the deck, install a new window, and any number of those things you want to be done to your property. Every single thing I asked him to do would be followed by a fax from him, noting exactly what was to be done, the price, a signature line, and date. The first time he did this, he said, "You're a lawyer, so you probably know a lot more about this than me." "No," I said, "You are doing precisely what any lawyer would tell his client." *This* was a contractor who never had to waste his time, or mine, discussing misunderstandings or memory lapses. If this seems like simple common sense, it is. Why doesn't everybody do it?

"But I distinctly remember." These words are often the prelude to a lawsuit. Elephants may have great memories, but elephants can't form contracts and start businesses; so unless you and your partner-to-be are elephants, consider this: your recollection of something in the past, just as that of your partner, is subject to human frailty. Any business lawyer can tell you that there are occasions where each opponent appears to be telling the absolute truth, but each version is completely opposite. And, in truth, if each opponent took a polygraph test, both would pass because each one sincerely *believes* his or her version of the agreement. Contracts don't mean that two people distrust one another. It means that both people prefer to be guided by good planning and the written word rather than by their ability to argue.

Contracts keep friendships. "But counselor, this is my brother (sister, best friend, etc.). We don't need a written contract." Any good lawyer will advise that a written contract is especially important for people who are related or close friends. Suppose two brothers have a serious disagreement down the road. If one is able to present the business agreement to the other, he can say, "Didn't we cover this at paragraph 9, section 3, when we started the business?" Remember the story I told about the 10 friends who started the food company? I understand from my friend that the individuals who formed the business are no longer friends. *APT Alert: Practice* A well-written contract will cover the vast number of possibilities that can come up in a business. But having a partner goes beyond the written contract. I discuss the *art of partnering* in the next section.

Shared Ownership Concerns: The Art of Partnering

"It's my way or the highway." Cute phrase. But if you enter into a multiple ownership business arrangement, forget that phrase. A good partnership, just like a good marriage, doesn't just happen. It needs to be *worked at*. There are a host of skills that you need to develop if you are to have a successful partnership. Notice that I say you "need" to develop these skills; it is not optional. The good news is that they are great skills to learn if you don't already have them, and they will enhance your position as a leader, whether you have partners or not. *APT Alert*: The following skills have to do with **attitude:**

Negotiation skills: A good negotiator knows that both sides have to win. If you manage to drive through your point in such a way that you completely win, you will both lose eventually, especially if you are negotiating with a partner. If you are on your own, you decide on a course of action and do it. With a partner, you have to get him or her to agree, to come around to your way of thinking. And if you're smart, you will not only talk, but listen. Consider the startling possibility that your partner may have a better idea.

Courtesy: Notice how the simple courtesies of life make the day much better. When someone holds a door for you, you automatically say "thank you." When you wave another motorist on to merge in front of you, he or she will wave back a thanks. We do this all the time with strangers, but we often forget to be courteous to those who are close. Your partner should constantly hear from you "please" and "thank you." So should your employees! Close proximity breeds a familiarity that doesn't often allow for the courtesies that you would extend to an outsider. Courtesies that you give have a way of coming back to you in a pleasant way. (Note: this includes the partnership of *marriage!*)

Praise: People love to be praised, and so does your partner. What happens when people are praised? They tend to like the person praising them. Do you want your partner to like you? Give praise when it is due. It will repay you dearly. But praise without sincerity can look like something else: manipulation. We have all encountered people who lavish so much praise that it makes you wonder what's up. On my blog, *The Moran Report,* I often receive a comment that praises me so highly I think I should have a column in *The New York Times.* I then look to the URL from which the praise comes from: diet programs, work-from-home schemes pornography websites, and, my favorite, a pole dancing school. They want me to leave their words on my site just so their sites turn up on search engines. Cute.

Patience: Do not allow yourself to get "plugged in" by something your partner does, even though it may well deserve your upset. Here you must exercise a great amount of skill in short-circuiting your anger and, if you do, you will keep the partnership healthy; but if you don't, irreparable damage can occur, your plans can be wrecked, your old friendship ruined, and your business in a shambles, all because you chose to pop off when you should have shut up. Knowing when to shut up is one of life's most neglected skills. A burst of negative emotion can linger for years, or forever, and will hold its power long after the reason for the outburst is forgotten. The most painful thing in the world is having somebody jump down your throat. Just shut up!

Openness: Invariably your partner will come up with an idea or will do something with which you completely disagree. Go a step beyond patience. Calm reflection, best done overnight, may result in a morning discovery—that your partner really had a good idea after all. I was in a peer advisory group once, and one of the group members could not seem to get anything that people were saying to him about an issue that he brought up and for which he was seeking advice. He was as open as a clam, and we all gradually realized that he was totally resistant to any ideas, other than his own. I'm glad he was not my partner. When your partner comes up with an idea, especially if he or she is enthusiastic about it, the most relationship-damaging thing you can do is shoot it down. We have all experienced dumb ideas, whether from a partner, an employee, or a fellow board member. The way to handle a dumb idea, especially when coming from a partner, is to ask questions. This will give you information to discuss THE NEXT DAY (no, not on the spot). You can then jot down a few more questions and be prepared to have an adult discussion. By the next day, your partner may have realized the idea was dumb—without your having to say so.

Honesty: Don't let something fester. At an appropriate time, schedule a meeting with your partner to express your concern. Thomas Jefferson said, "Honesty is the first chapter of the book of wisdom." If you think your partner's plans for a three-week vacation during a very busy time is not a good idea, you need to be honest and say so. As with all good communication, begin with questions. For example, "Do you think our staff can do without you during that time?" If you aren't out in the open about things, problems will become sublimated into your subconscious list of negatives, and eventually you will begin to resent your partner—all because you weren't open to begin with. The late political writer William Safire was once asked if he thought that poor communication was caused by ignorance or apathy. "I don't know, and I don't care," said Safire. His humor made the point. Both ignorance and apathy can kill honest communication.

Trust: Trust is often thought of as a result of something. "Let me see if I can trust this guy based on what he does." Trust is also a *decision,* a decision on your part that you will trust your partner as a default way of thinking. Negative interpretations of something can lead to paranoia which, in turn, reinforces negative interpretations. I am not talking about putting on blinders and failing to pay attention to what is going on. The trustees of

Orange County, California put unwavering trust in the county treasurer. He invested county funds in financial derivatives, and he turned the once wealthy Orange County into an economic basket case. Trust is an important dimension to your relationship with your partner, but trust includes realistic thinking. I knew a guy who ran a restaurant and put his implicit trust in his managing bartender. One night, having forgotten something, my friend returned to the restaurant just after closing time. There was his trusted bartender, loading cases of wine into the trunk of his car. Trust should never trump common sense, and if you find that you cannot trust your partner, it's time to start thinking about winding up the partnership rather than labor on constantly looking over your shoulder.

Respect: Show respect for your partner even when out of earshot. Never criticize your partner in front of other employees. If an employee comes to you and says, "Joe did it again," take time to get a detailed explanation, without taking sides with the employee, and end it by saying that you will speak with Joe about the issue. Also show respect for your partner when you go home and review the day with your spouse. Show respect, and it will be returned to you. Don't show it, and the insult will breed like a virus.

Keep yourself, and your partner, trained: I try to avoid being didactic, but I present this to you as a truism: only an outside influence can change adult behavior. By outside influence, I mean a professional trainer, coach, or consultant. Many businesses, especially small ones, overlook the importance of keeping management trained, including you. If you practice the skills I have been talking about in this section, wouldn't it be nice if your partner practiced them as well? Too many business owners think that training is something for subordinates and that the owner and other managers can handle the teaching. Big mistake. Training should be a part of your annual budget. Regular management training is essential to the health of any business. I will discuss more about management and employee training in Chapter 7.

Chapter 5 Summary

In this chapter I discussed the following:

- The different ways of doing business: sole propri-etorship, partnership, corporation, and limited liabil-ity company (LLC)
- Benefits of sole ownership
- Benefits of shared ownership
- Shared ownership concerns: legal issues
- The need for a business agreement
- Shared ownership concerns: the art of partnering

CHAPTER 6

Locating Your Business

APT Principal: Practice

Own or Rent

My accountant for my old company gave me some very sage advice. If possible, buy the building you will occupy because it will help fund your future. I bought a 3,000-square-foot building in 1991, after 10 years in business, for $135,000. To allow for expansion, I bought an adjacent building in 1997 for $125,000. I sold my company in 2000 but kept the buildings and rented them out. They are now worth over $800,000, even in a tough real estate market, and are fully rented. Very good advice indeed.

Obviously, the decision to buy or rent must be guided by the needs of your particular business. If your business requires an urban setting in a big city, buying may be out of the question. But even in a large city, an office condominium is worth considering. Commercial real estate is a wonderfully leveraged investment. You depreciate the asset as it grows in value, all the while paying rent to yourself or taking in additional rental income. Warning: real estate values fluctuate, as we all learned from the Great Financial Meltdown. If you're thinking that you can buy a building or condo and "flip" it for a profit if things don't work out, you need an **attitude** check. Think long term. Eliminate the word *flip* from your vocabulary when thinking real estate. But there are bargains out there, as there always are in a down market. Owning a building also gives you a lot of flexibility. If you need to expand, you could add a wing or build another floor. If you have space left over for rental, this will not only keep down your operating costs, but it will also enable you to rent to a tenant who may be helpful for your operation.

If you do purchase, I don't recommend doing it in the name of your existing business, but rather form a separate corporation or LLC. If you sell your business, your real estate is a separate negotiation. Your buyer may intend to relocate anyway, so owning it separately will yield you a much better profit instead of "bundling" it with the sale of your business. When I sold my company, the purchaser stayed on as a sole tenant for five years.

High or Low Profile

Obviously, I can't determine whether you need a glitzy location or a small office over a garage. Personal preference has much to do with it—probably too much. Business decisions should be rational first, emotional second. The kind of business you are in should dictate the parameters of your location. You might find an absolutely delightful building or condo, but in an area totally incompatible with your needs. Consider the following guide for types of businesses and whether they require a high or low profile.

High profile: Good visibility, traffic, parking, and quality construction. Depending on your exact business and your marketing plan, your requirements can vary greatly from another company in a similar business. For example, if you have a narrowly focused business, such as vehicular traffic consulting, go for low profile; they will find you in a directory or through Google. My former business, legal publishing and research, was conducted by phone and mail, but I opted for a high profile—one mile from a major court complex and across the street from a large restaurant that was heavily patronized by lawyers and judges. Every time they looked out the window they would see my company's name. I actually had walk-in business, something I had never conceived of when I started the company.

The following list of types of businesses is by no means exhaustive, but it is intended to assist your thinking.

High Profile

Accounting firm
Advertising agency
Antique dealership
Art gallery
Consulting firm
Dentist office
Insurance agency
Investment firm
Law firm
Photo studio
Real estate brokerage
Restaurant

Retail store
Title insurance company
Veterinary office

Low profile: You have to look for it to find it. Low profile does not mean ugly. If your business is one that would not benefit from a large public exposure, the savings achieved by a lower rent space are entirely justified. Low profile can include space in an industrial zoned area.

The following are some businesses that are appropriate for low-profile locations:

Food brokers
Graphic design firm (unless you have a significant clientele among consumers)
Industry publications
Internet service providers
Manufacturing facilities
Metal brokers
Newsletters
Research companies
Trade magazines
Wholesale distributors

The above businesses do not operate by customer or vehicular traffic. They get business by people searching them out, unlike a restaurant, which needs to be highly visible. The decision to locate in a high- or low-profile setting should be dictated by marketing considerations: Do you want or need to have high public exposure?

Choosing a Location: A Checklist

Caution: Do not let emotion dictate your location decision in any way. The following list of factors should be your guide. I recommend photocopying this list and using it while looking for a location. (Yes, this is an exception to the copyright notice in the front of the book.)

Importance to Your Business

Factor: a. Very important; b. Somewhat important; c. Not at all important. Insert a, b or c next to each factor.

Aesthetic appeal

Age of building

Cost

Ease of access

Ease of maintenance

Ease of wiring for computers and other equipment

Flexible lease or purchase options

Future expandability

High public visibility

Need for repairs

On-site storage

One level

Parking

Pedestrian traffic

> Proximity to amenities for employees (nearby deli?)
> Proximity to major roads or public transportation
> Proximity to support businesses such as printing
> Safety
> Stability (Will you be able to stay there a long time?)
> Subdividable (able to sublet to others?)
> Utility costs

By using a list of factors as outlined above, you will make your decision based on needs, not an emotional reaction to a pretty building. I had a friend with a small graphic design business who dealt primarily with corporate customers and didn't need a high-profile location. She found a place on a main road with a beautiful lake behind it, including ducks and swans and a gorgeous view. The rental costs were very high; given its location, it would have been a perfect spot for a restaurant. The rent was so high, in fact, that she would need to bring in about 20 percent more business just to crack the monthly nut. Details be damned! She threw out any financial considerations because she freaked out over the ducks and swans. She would have been better served by renting a modest place in a back-office area and splashing her computer with pretty, rotating screen savers—including ducks and swans.

Working from Home

Working out of your own house or apartment has tremendous appeal for some people. Every time you turn on the radio, you hear an ad pushing this or that work-from-home business. Working from your home can have definite advantages, especially financial ones.

It can also suck.

Advantages of Working from Home

Working from home has one immediate advantage: low overhead expense. Not only do you forego rent or an additional mortgage payment, but you can legitimately write off part of your home expenses for business use on your tax return. Caution: the IRS gets very squirrely about home-office deductions. Be conservative, and be guided by your accountant. A rule to live by: never mess with the IRS.

There are other money-saving realities of working from home: save on gas; save on dry-cleaning (business attire is required only if a client comes to visit); and you save on all of the expenses of maintaining an off-premises business, such as utilities, repairs, landscaping, snow removal, etc., because they are already factored into your home maintenance costs. Working from home also has distinct advantages, depending on your own needs. If you are a single parent, being there for your kids at the beginning or end of the school day is a gift for you and your kids. Waiting for the repairman—a reality of life. A broken refrigerator, washer, dryer, or a leaking roof all need attention, and your presence is required. You don't need to take time off from the office because you are *in* your office. Some aspects of your personal life are also enhanced by working out of the house. You can hit the treadmill at mid-day, and who is to notice?

I won't list all of the possible of types of businesses and professions that can be conducted from home because they are obvious—to you. Only you can decide if your home is the appropriate venue for your business or practice. Some businesses can start from home and migrate to a new location when circumstances, and budget, dictate. Whether the physical design of your home allows for appropriate meetings with clients is a key consideration. But, if your business is one that requires no specific location for meeting with people, you're in luck. Very important: make sure to check your local zoning codes to make certain that your business is appropriate for running out of a residence. If you see virtually no clients at all, you don't have a problem. But some professions that are client intensive are traditional occupations for a zoning blessing, even in a residential area, such as professional practices. This varies from state to state and from town to town, but the usual list of in-home business providers that are okay with the zoning folks include physicians, dentists, chiropractors, accountants, lawyers, and so on. And the list goes on. Check with your town hall. It's easier to call them than to fight them.

Challenges of Working from Home

I say *challenges,* not disadvantages, because whether you can live and work with these details is entirely personal. I am a writer and, like most writers, I work from my home. Before I sold my company, I went to an office every day, so I have some serious perspective on the advantages and challenges of working at home. I've done both.

Some writers, like the deservedly rich and famous novelist Nelson DeMille, found that working from his house (large as it is) didn't suit him, so he goes to an office every day to do his writing. Nelson also does not use a computer but does all his writing on yellow pads for transcription by a secretary. That he writes on yellow pads has nothing to do with the subject of working from home, but I thought I'd share that tidbit with you. Different strokes for different folks.

Distractions

Distractions are the biggest challenge of working where you live. There are always chores that scream at you to drop work and handle them. In bad weather, I often get my half-hour exercise by walking around my big old house. Every room I walk through reminds me of a chore that I should get to—165-year-old houses are like that. It's easy to forget that I am at work. Often I get my exercise on a treadmill while watching a video course on classical music appreciation or some other subject that I want to learn more about. I don't consider this a distraction, but rather an important part of my day devoted to health—physical and mental. Fortunately, my house includes a whole separate wing that I use for my office and storage. It used to be a maid's quarters. But your needs will be determined by your physical realities. As for those numerous tasks that really are nothing more than distractions, there is one best way to handle them: write them down and schedule a time to handle them. I discuss time management in detail in Chapter 8.

Discipline

Working from home does not—should not—mean that you get to sleep late and go to your home office in your pajamas. Note: this is a personal opinion. I prefer to get up, shower, and get dressed just as if I were heading out to an office, although without a tie. Some work-at-homers will even insist on wearing a dress shirt and tie, or a business suit for a woman. It is a reminder that you're at work. Just as you plan your day at the office, you need to plan your day at your home office. Pick a time to *show up* in your home office, a time to go to lunch and, especially, a time to "go home." Consider your home office a place to go and, just as important, a place to leave. Your family is, or should be, the most important thing in your life. Don't burden them with your office work by *staying late* and neglecting them; but during working hours make sure they recognize that you are at work, not just in a different place in the house. If you're just starting out and your house does not allow for a separate office, you will need to make a space in the house do "double-duty." You need to do whatever works. But I strongly recommend that your double-duty space be closed up or covered after your workday, or your workday will never end. Imagine sitting with your spouse and kids, watching TV or catching up on reading, and feeling guilty about not sitting at your desk working. If this happens to you, go out now and rent an office.

Working from home can be a great way to conduct a business, if appropriate to your circumstances. Just recognize that you need to have the right **attitude,** and institute the right **practices** to pull it off. Otherwise, you'll just be a stay-at-home who gets a lot of laundry and other chores done, but very little business.

Coworking – A Modern Alternative to Working from Home

We are social animals, in varying degrees. Human beings, as a general rule, like to interact with other people. We like to chat, discuss ball scores, exchange ideas, and tell jokes. We like to say "good morning," good night," and "have a nice weekend." We are empowered by other people, and we, in turn, empower them. It is no wonder that one of the most rigorous forms of punishment is to put a prisoner in solitary confinement, depriving the person of interaction with other human beings. Some consider solitary confinement to be cruel and unusual punishment. When you work from home you miss the constant company of other people. I sometimes run to the door when the UPS truck pulls up just so I can have a chat with the driver.

Small businesses, especially one person operations, can benefit from a new way of renting office space. Coworking means a desk, a possibly prestigious address, perhaps conference space, and most important, the opportunity to mingle with other small business and professional people. While there is more cost than working from home, the rents tend to be reasonable with no long term commitment, usually a month to month rental. The offerings for these spaces vary quite a bit, from just a desk, to the use of a conference room, high speed Internet hookup and WiFi. There may be a communal kitchen with coffee service. Some coworking locations even offer secretarial and reception capabilities.

Coworking facilities are usually found in densely populated areas. To see what offerings are out there, simply Google "coworking" and your town. If you fit the profile – a solo business person or professional, coworking may be an excellent solution for you.

Chapter 6 Summary

In this chapter I discussed the following:

- The location of your business
- Whether you should buy or rent
- High- and low-profile locations
- Types of businesses suitable for high or low profile
- How to choose a location
- The benefits and challenges of working from home
- Coworking – a modern alternative to working from home

CHAPTER 7

Employees are the Foundation for Your Business

APT Principle: Practice

Hiring the Right People

If you don't think that hiring talented employees is a Best Practice, then you should stop reading now because you are not really serious about the business of running a business. Too many employers treat hiring as a necessary annoyance and hurry through the process to get it over with. Hiring the right people can breathe life into your business plan and your business itself. The opposite is also true: hire the wrong people and your plans can be dashed. Do not delegate hiring, no matter how minor the position. Obviously, depending on the size of your organization, you may need to have some initial screening done by others, but the final decision is yours. If you administer a test, or have a lengthy application that needs to be filled out, delegate someone to oversee this process. I wish I could say otherwise, but hiring people isn't easy. Like anything well executed, you need to plan, to go through the necessary procedures, and to make a decision based on reason, not emotion.

Recruiting

After the great economic slowdown that began in 2007, job growth has been slower than normal for an economic recovery. Some think that job growth will be anemic for many years to come. After the terrible business downturn, many organizations that had to lay off employees have chosen to purchase productivity-enhancing technology, rather than simply start hiring as business starts to pick up. As consumers start to spend and businesses start to recover, it becomes necessary to hire. Many business owners are putting off hiring until the last minute because the future looks cloudy. The uncertainty of costs under the new health care plan is another impediment to robust job growth, as well as uncertainty about changing regulatory burdens and, of course, taxes. The bottom line: there are a lot of people out there—good people— who can propel your business to new heights. Your job is to find them.

Being Specific about Your Hiring Needs

Whether you are writing a job posting or spreading the word among your contacts, it is just plain stupid to be vague about the job opening. If it's entry level, say so. I once advertised for an editorial assistant, a typical entry-level job in publishing. I wasn't specific enough that it was entry level, and I spent long hours combing through résumés of PhDs who apparently thought the job was for a senior editor. If the job is high level, say so also. You are wasting your time and that of the job seeker if you don't communicate what you want.

Getting Résumés

In times of economic trouble, getting résumés to your mailroom is the easy part. Craigslist.com has become a category killer for classified ads. It is credited, if that isn't a poor choice of words, with putting major and local newspapers out of business in California because so much of the classified ad revenue migrated from the newspapers to Craigslist. It is widely used, probably because it's free to post job openings. You will be amazed how many responses you get to a posting on craigslist.com. Smart job hunters make it widely known among friends to help them by being on the lookout for any openings, and this can result in your job posting becoming *viral* by word of mouth. Craigslist is a no-brainer. Depending on the position that you have available, you may also want to investigate paid job listing sites, like monster.com. You can also use the phenomenon of social networking to get the word out. Don't ignore Twitter, Facebook, or LinkedIn. Imagine tweeting "Job opening for licensed property insurance agent on Long Island," followed by a link to your website. That tweet can go viral within a matter of hours. Besides lists and social networking media, don't ignore word of mouth recruiting; make it known to your entire circle of friends and contacts that you have an opening. There is no single magic bullet. Use multiple approaches, and you will have no problem getting qualified applicants.

Cover letters and résumés are an applicant's opportunity to get your attention and capture your interest. As important as these documents are, it's amazing how many job-seekers pay so little attention to getting it right. There are books, seminars, and articles on the Internet about the dos and don'ts of résumé writing. As a prospective employer, you have every right to expect that both the cover letter and résumé will be executed perfectly. Not *well* executed. *Perfectly* executed. Spelling errors, typos, and poor grammar tell a lot about the job seeker. Do you expect that, once hired, this person is suddenly going to stop making mistakes? As a publisher, I was especially critical of the submitted written word. Even one mistake would take the seeker out of contention. A cover letter and résumé are the most important project on the applicant's desk, and if that job is botched, think about how the applicant would handle an important project or assignment. Don't think that you are being overly hard-assed about this. The job seeker has the opportunity to proofread the résumé and to get input from friends. The word "whoops" doesn't cut it in the world of résumés.

Résumé Red Flags

Reading a résumé requires a lot of common sense, not to mention a good dose of a caffeinated beverage, but there are some critical issues that you should tune your antenna to: the résumé itself. As discussed above, if the résumé is covered with mistakes, don't assume that the mistakes will magically go away when you hire the person. Preparing a résumé is an applicant's first opportunity to put his best foot forward, and if that foot has the wrong shoe on it, trash the résumé.

Job-hopping. I once read a résumé where the applicant listed a new job every year for 12 years. My imagination couldn't come up with a valid reason for changing jobs once a year, so I tossed the résumé. There is no magic formula for how many years a person should remain on a job, but don't expect the job-hopping to stop with you. Whether it's a problem with attention span, an inability to get along with others, or simply restiveness, a job-hopper is not someone you want to work for you. So, what is the right number? I don't know; it's your call. But 12 jobs in 12 years? Hop away.

Too much variation in jobs. He tried marketing for a while, then to moved to finance, followed up by a stint in IT, and then went on to the restaurant industry. What's going on? There may be a good reason that a person has held many different jobs; it could show creativity or ambition. I wouldn't toss a résumé based on these criteria alone, but it is a red flag. If you choose to interview the applicant, delve into his ever-changing career plan.

Total lack of experience. This is the problem for the applicant who is just out of school. I list it as a red flag because you should be concerned, but I don't consider lack of job experience for an entry-level person to be an automatic exclusion. Everybody has to start somewhere, but it is your job to determine if your business will be the starting place. At minimum, you know that a person lacking in experience will require a lot of training and mentoring. On the positive side, an inexperienced applicant will be trained according to your requirements, and you will not have to untrain bad habits. If you see that the applicant had interesting experiences during her time in school, you may consider an interview. If the applicant did her homework, she would have listed every extra-curricular activity as if it were a job. Volunteer activities, sports, school club memberships—all of these could indicate a flower about to bloom. Oh yes, don't forget grades if academic achievement is a requirement. Ask for a transcript before you set up an interview. I'm not suggesting that a job applicant might lie on a résumé, but stranger things have happened.

The unemployed applicant. Some businesses have a policy of not hiring anyone who is unemployed. This is just plain stupid. If a person is unemployed, obviously you want to know the story. Was the person fired? How long has he or she been unemployed? As I write this, the government, in its unflagging belief that the free market cannot be left to its own devices, may soon get into the act. The administration is talking about making it a *discriminatory* labor practice to refuse to hire the unemployed. If this becomes law, you won't even be able to ask questions about the period of unemployment, which shows the insanity of such a proposal. Would you be required to file a federal affidavit under oath for every résumé you look at, swearing that you did not grant an interview for other than the reason that the person is unemployed? The federal government will do what it does best (worst?) and write rules and regulations to solve a perceived problem, but my point is that refusing to hire someone simply because that person is unemployed is a bad business practice. There are a lot of talented people out there who have lost their jobs because of economic conditions. Employment status should not be an automatic trigger to refuse to interview someone.

The Interview

Most experienced business and professional people that I know think they're David Frost or Barbara Walters when they interview someone. "I have had enough years under my belt to be a good judge of character based on an interview alone." Baloney. An interview is a surface-level exchange, and how much you can tell about someone by talking across a desk is limited. The formal job interview is important, but don't think it means everything. Interviewees are on their best behavior, wanting to impress you, and you're on your best behavior, wanting to impress the interviewees. It's like asking a girl to dance. The fact that she is pretty, laughs at your jokes, and carries on a good conversation does not necessarily mean you should get married. What about shy people? Shy people should not be shy on an interview, right? Nonsense—shy people are shy, and some make terrific employees. It depends on the job. If it's a sales position, shyness might be a real detriment. But what about an editorial assistant, a bookkeeper, a file clerk, or a computer technician? Some of my best employees were extremely shy but did a great job. An interview is a theatrical situation, with the actors playing their parts, including you. Don't expect too much of it. A Best Practice is to have the applicant interviewed by other key employees. They might see something that you missed. Always—*always*—ask the applicant why he left each job. This is critical because the answers might tell you a lot about the person. And learn you will because you are going to interview the people for whom he once worked. More about this below in the references section.

The most important thing about interviewing is this: DON'T HIRE YOURSELF. A good organization has a variety of characters, with different personalities and idiosyncrasies, and it's a mistake to think that all of your employees should have the same traits as you. I discuss this in more detail shortly. Too many "mini-mes" can make for a very weird organization.

References: The Gold Standard of Hiring

Are you a good judge of character? Of course you are; we all think we are. But experience has taught me that sometimes I can be a lousy judge of character, and I have made some bone-headed hiring decisions just because I liked the applicant. Be humble, admit your social fallibility, and talk to prior employers, the people for whom the applicants actually worked. If the applicant refuses to give references, politely, and for obvious reasons, end the interview. If former employers have something good to say, they will say it. Do call the references and interview them. People worry about legal liability for a host of things, and a lawsuit for defamation of character is one of them. Such people will either risk the legal liability and tell you exactly why they fired your applicant or will say "No comment." "No comment" is a big comment. Talking to former employers will tell you much more about an applicant than you will ever get from an interview. But don't be overly swayed by positive comments and praise. Consider the possibility that a former employer had to let go of the person because he, the employer screwed up the business and had to lay off people because of it. To assuage his guilt, he might overly praise the applicant because he really wants to help the applicant get a job (to replace the one he lost). Be skeptical and balanced when you talk to references. Good people have been fired for bad reasons. Just ask John Sculley, the guy who fired Steve Jobs from Apple. Whoops!

Hiring is critical because firing (and replacing) is difficult. Now we will look at the **attitude**s, **practices,** and **technology** that you should consider in staffing your business.

Training: A Best Practice

I don't want to overstress the obvious here, but hiring people to do a job that they don't know how to do is like coaching a team without training them in the sport. Some jobs can be assigned to employees who are already trained in a special occupation, such as a computer programmer, a bookkeeper, or a technician. But even when you hire someone who comes to the job with specialized skills, you still need to train that person in the culture, rules, and needs of your organization. This is simple stuff, but it is important nevertheless because you have designed it that way, including how to answer the phone. "XYZ Corporation. This is Phil. How may I help you?" Simple things like that. People aren't born with such knowledge; they must be trained to be a part of *your* business.

Are you a good trainer? Do you have key employees who are good trainers? If your answer is an honest "no," that doesn't mean that you don't have to provide training. It means you have to hire outside help. There are coaches and consultants who specialize in training employees and you are still key to the process because they will ask you to help design the curriculum for training, specific to your organization. If you are a small business and don't hire new employees that often, the training consultant's job will be to train you, and perhaps some key employees, to do the training using the curriculum that you helped develop.

Outside Trainers and Training Programs

Training adults, like teaching kids, is a specialized field for which not everyone is suited, including some who are in the field. Training requires energy, personality, attention to detail, and brains. It is an occupation in itself, and that's why I have a strong bias toward using outside training organizations in addition to the training that you and your current staff provide. Training is not a one-time seminar or program but a continual process. Typically, you can't find business trainers in the phone book, but there are places to go for help. The American Society for Training and Development (ASTD) claims to be the world's largest professional association dedicated to the training and development community. Founded in 1944, it has over 70,000 members. Its extensive website is found at www.astd.org. On that site you can peruse the types of training programs that are offered by members in your area.

Myers-Briggs

I hired trainers for various programs over the years. By far, one of the best was the famous Myers-Briggs program, called MBTI for Myers-Briggs Type Indicator. We each have basic core personality types, although we all like to think we're unique. Knowing your personality profile and the profile of those with whom you work every day is what Myers-Briggs is all about. The idea is to isolate what personality type you are, as well as your employees. The primary component is an assessment questionnaire designed to measure psychological preferences that people use to perceive the world and make decisions. The developers of the program were Katharine Cook Briggs and her daughter, Isabel Briggs Myers, basing their work on the book by the influential psychologist Carl Jung, *Psychological Types*. The premise behind the theory is that much of our behavior is actually quite orderly and consistent because of the differences in the ways individuals prefer to use their perception and judgment. It's not about aptitude but rather individual preferences that are hard wired into our personalities. The test measures your preferences toward the following:

- Extroversion (E) versus Introversion (I)
- Sensing (S) versus Intuition (N)
- Thinking (T) versus Feeling (F)
- Judgment (J) versus Perception (P)

At the end of the test, you get labeled (nobody likes to be labeled, but roll with it). So, the boss might be an ESTJ (Extroverted, Sensing, Thinking, and a Judgment maker) and the copy boy an INFP (Introverted, Intuitive,

Feeling, and Perceptive). If this sounds like fun, it is, but it's a lot more than that. Other than relying on my own preconceptions, I never had more awareness of myself and my relationship with my employees than I did after a Myers-Briggs program. Not only did I have better awareness, but I also learned that I needed to act a certain way with some employees because of their profiles. For example, don't yell at an INFP; it won't get you anywhere. You can take the program online (of course), but I strongly recommend that you spend the money and hire a facilitator skilled in presenting and administering the Myers-Briggs program. More information can be found at the website of the Myers-Briggs Foundation, www.myersbriggs.org.

Employee Handbook

Yes, you should have an employee handbook setting forth all of the practices and procedures of your company relating to its people. Included in the handbook should be sick leave and vacation policies, benefits, including health insurance, a 401(k) or other retirement program if you have one, and your policy concerning inappropriate behavior. You should consult with your attorney on this, but you will probably be told that the handbook should not be written as a contract, but only a set of general guidelines; and a statement to that effect should be right at the beginning of the manual. If the document is found to be a contract by a court, you could lose all legal flexibility. For example, if you list a number of reasons for termination, and you fire someone for a reason not on the list, you could be found to have breached a contract.

Job Manual for Each Position

A job manual is a document that describes in detail just what a particular position involves. This Best Practice can be invaluable if an employee leaves for any reason. The person you hire as a replacement will have a guide for the position. It is essential that the person who writes the manual be the employee who actually holds the position because only that person really knows what the job entails. Most companies, in my experience, do not have job manuals, and this is a big mistake. Besides the obvious benefit of a smooth transition for replacements, having each employee write his or her own manual is a great exercise in focusing the employee on just what the job is. You will be amazed at the disconnect between what you think the job is and what your employee thinks.

There is one problem with the job manual: employees hate to write it. But it should be a requirement, a project, and like any project, it needs to be scheduled and given a firm deadline. You should take the job manual seriously, and communicate this to your employees by requiring that they revisit and update the manual every six months. Job details change, and the manual needs to change accordingly. A well-written job manual for each position in your organization will prove to be a core component of your company's structure. Before my wife Lynda joined my company as vice president, I had never heard of a job manual. She instituted it and urged, cajoled, and made life difficult for people until they got it done. When we sold our company, the buyer was delighted that we had accomplished this project.

Chapter 7 Summary

In this chapter I discussed the following:

- Hiring the right people
- Recruiting
- Being specific about your expectations
- Getting résumés
- Recognizing résumé red flags
- Conducting the job interview
- References
- Training
- Myers-Briggs
- Employee Handbook
- Writing a job manual for each position

CHAPTER 8

Time Management

APT Principles: Attitude, Practices, and Technology

I start this chapter with a promise: I'm going to show you how to create more time. No, you didn't misread that sentence. I am literally going to show you not only how to manage time, but also how to manufacture more of it. I mean it. Before you ask for your money back on this book, please read on.

What is time?

This is a business book, not a philosophical treatise, but it helps to ground our thinking by taking a look at exactly what we are talking about. Philosophers have been having a ball with the concept of time for a long, well, time. The Greek philosopher Parmenides believed that reality is timeless and never changes. Heraclitus, another Greek philosopher, believed that reality is a constant state of change.

I'm going with Heraclitus, and I think you will, too. Here's why. I suggest that a working definition of time that we can all live with must not be some theory that we cannot understand; rather, it should be grounded in a reality that we can easily conceive of. I think the issue, as a practical matter, is more a function of neurology or psychology than of metaphysics. So here is my working definition: time is what we *perceive* as a constantly changing reality, where we remember what we perceived in the past, actually perceive what's happening now, and imagine what will happen in the future based on our memories and perceptions. That's it; nothing really complicated. The main point is that we *perceive* time with our senses and mind, as a linear progression of events. So, is time perception? Yes, at least for my working definition. As I write this, I have just read about a group of scientists, using a particle accelerator, who discovered that a subatomic particle called a *neutrino* can actually go faster than the speed of light. This means that Einstein's formula $E=MC^2$ (energy = mass times the speed of light squared) is wrong, and if it's wrong, all of our formulas describing the physical world for the last 100 years have to be rewritten. It also means that if the speed of light can be exceeded, then the possibility of going backward in time is possible, really screwing up our knowledge of this thing called time. But that's okay. Small errors were found on further study, and Einstein's formula is safe and sound. The scientific and philosophical debate is fascinating and fun, but it's not going to help you meet payroll.

Let's stipulate that there are 365 days in a year, 24 hours in a day, and 60 minutes in an hour. That's it; that's all we get. But I'm not going to renege on my promise to show you how to make more time. What I will do is make the time longer, especially those minutes and hours. It's all about PERCEPTION.

If I'm heating something in the microwave for two minutes, it's no big deal. The time flies by, and I'm ready to eat or drink what's in the oven. On the other hand, the last two minutes of a New York Jets game takes, in my perception as a New York Jets fan, about an hour. Think about these short increments of time and how your perception varies depending on your circumstances. You're late for an important meeting, and the traffic light turns red. Although it may be red for only a minute, it seems to you like an eternity. Perception. When you're young, the summer seemed to go on forever. When you get older, it seems like you are planting flowers one day and raking leaves the next. Time *seems* to go faster the older one gets. But does it really go faster? Remember 365 days a year, 24 hours in a day, and so on? It's the same amount of time; we just *perceive* it differently depending on many different circumstances.

Manufacturing Time by Changing Your Perception of it

No, I'm not going to set forth some beliefs that I ask you to buy; I'm not asking you to change your opinion of anything, including the concept of time; nor am I asking you to take anything on faith. What I'm suggesting is that you take actions that will actually give you more time by *shifting your perception*. We can't change the actual amount of time, but we can change how we perceive it. It's not magic—I don't know, maybe it is—but *it works.* I'm asking you to help me identify those things that rob you of time—or what screws up your perception of it.

Time-Gnats and How to Kill Them

I hate gnats. They get in your hair, in your ear, fly up your nose, and the ones that miss you end up in your drink. At least mosquitoes let you know they're coming. Gnats steal pleasure from you; they take a pleasant summer evening and turn you into a crazy person slapping your own face. Gnats suck. They must die! *Time-gnats* must die, too. A time-gnat is a little beastie that robs your time, just like regular gnats ruin your party. Let's talk about time-gnats and learn how to kill them.

What is a time-gnat? A time-gnat is a sudden recollection of a chore that you need to do but have been putting off. It may be a phone call, a letter that needs writing, an e-mail that requires an answer, or any of those little things that we must do in life every day. Time-gnats don't fly up your nose or into your ear—they enter your head directly. Usually they are something unpleasant, something you put off because it's not agreeable, but they can also be simple, mundane tasks that are easily deferred. Time-gnats slow you down by causing you to be vaguely aware of them, while time speeds by, thereby giving you the perception that you are running out of time, that you don't have enough of it. Time gnats don't find their way into your appointment book or to-do list because they don't seem to be that important. THAT is the problem. That is what turns "something to do" into a time-gnat. So, instead of scheduling a time to handle the chore, you allow the gnat to stay in your head, buzzing around and screwing with your mind. A bunch of time-gnats in your head slows you down, actually steals time from you, and you can't even identify the little bastards, but they are there, in your head. Collectively, the gnats give you a sluggish feeling, causing you to say, "I know there's something I'm supposed to do, but I can't remember what." My favorite dramatic example of a time-gnat is in the movie *It's a Wonderful Life.* Remember how every time George Bailey (Jimmy Stewart) walked upstairs in his house, the banister post would come off in his hand? Jimmy Stewart's facial expression told you that a time-gnat just flew into his head. His face said, "I have to fix this one of these days."

Okay. Here's my biodegradable, environmentally sound, humane, and guaranteed way to kill time-gnats: WRITE THEM DOWN. Done, voila, dead as a doornail. You kill a time-gnat by writing it down. Here is the procedure (***APT Alert: Make this a practice***): Take an index card and write this across the top: *Dead Gnat File.* I prefer an index card because it's easily placed in an appointment book or wallet. If you're totally digital, make an electronic file for the same purpose. I prefer to scribble things down on paper. It's a Baby-Boomer thing. Recognize that many time-gnats are not very important, and that's one of the reasons you allow them to buzz around in your head instead of killing them by writing them down. Read your Dead Gnat File at least once a week and—this is important—transfer any dead gnat that becomes important from your Dead Gnat File to your to-do list, and schedule it for handling. As you transfer the gnat to your to-do list, cross it off the Dead Gnat File. (This, I promise, is fun.) Also cross out any dead gnats that are no longer of any importance. If it becomes important in the future, that means it has come alive, and you have to kill it again by writing it down again. Kill time-gnats immediately. When one enters your head, WRITE IT DOWN. Enjoy the vast amount of time you just created!

Let Your Desk Clean Itself

Your cluttered desk is a breeding ground for time-gnats. It's worse than that because you are only vaguely aware of what gnats lurk thereupon. I laugh when people tell me that they know where everything is amid the clutter on their desks. No, they don't, unless they're savants that can see through paper. I suggest to you that when stacking papers, by the time a pile gets three sheets deep, you haven't the foggiest idea what's there. It's ONE BIG TIME ROBBER.

Many people hate to clean off their desks. I do. All of those decisions: do I file this, act on it, throw it away? What to do? Besides all of the decisions, the effort is sheer drudgery, which is why we usually have cluttered desks. My old pal and former business coach Bob Shearer taught me this a few years ago. We would always meet in my office, and my desk was in plain sight, looking like the beginning of a revolution, missing only the burning barricades. He asked me how I felt about my mess of a desk, and I honestly told him (a) I hate it and (b) I don't know what to do about it because every time I clean it, the mess seems to return. He said, "Don't clean it; let it clean itself." Bob had a great sense of humor, so I assumed he was joking. He wasn't.

Here's how to let your desk clean itself. Warning: this might sound crazy, perhaps childish, even imbecilic, but what can be crazier, more childish, or more imbecilic than a desk that looks like a dumpster? You might want to do this when none of your employees are around, lest they call security, assuming the boss has suddenly lost his marbles. Reach out and grab the closest thing that's on your desk. It may be an unopened envelope, a paper clip, a coaster, an old theater ticket, or a magazine. Ask the object, OUT LOUD, "Where do you want to go?" I make you this promise: I have never picked up an object, which, when asked where it wanted to go, did not tell me. That crap on your desk knows where it belongs, and for every object that finds a home, *you have manufactured some more time.*

I respect you for reading this book, so I'm not going to insult your intelligence by asking you to take something on faith. I'm going to pick apart this "self-cleaning desk" procedure and see why it works. Believe me, it does work. Here's why: the *self-cleaning desk* is a game. Make it fun. When my desk allows itself to get cluttered (see, I'm shifting blame to the desk), I sometimes get angry and heap four-letter words on the object, as in : "What the %&@# are you doing here? Where do you want to go?" A game calls out to be played, and this is true with the *self-cleaning desk.* The drudgery of deciding what to do with all that stuff gets carried forward because we're hardwired to complete games that we started. It can be played silently, with you *thinking* at the object, "Where do you want to go?" But that's no fun. Talk to the stuff. The game is played alongside traditional organization techniques. Barbara Hemphill, founder of the Taming the Paper Tiger organizing system, suggests that for each object you touch, you make a decision using the acronym FAT: File, Act, or Toss. The Act stuff—items that require attention—then go into an A, B, or C file, depending on their importance. Don't worry. The stuff on your desk will tell you. I will discuss Barbara Hemphill and the Paper Tiger in more detail later in the chapter on technology. Barbara is also the founder of the Productive Environment Process, an organization that includes teams of people known as Certified Productive Environment Specialists. See www. productiveenvironment.com. They use a variety of tools, including the Paper Tiger, to get businesses organized. I bet she rotates her car's tires every three months!

Your clean desk will reinforce your commitment to keep it that way because of the wonderful experience that you have created *more time*. Let the game begin! When you look at your clean desk, you will have an amazing feeling that all of a sudden you have more time. That's because you do, and your desk created it for you.

Getting in Shape: Create Time

Okay, okay. I realize that I am placing myself in the pantheon of pains in the ass who tell you to exercise more, but this really is important. Your physical health and energy have a direct impact on the way time proceeds. Let's face it: when you're tired, time drags, and you're not productive. When you have energy and a clear head, you can fit multiple tasks into a given period. Like anything worthwhile, exercise needs to be scheduled. As I said before, I hate to exercise. When I do, however, the good feeling I get afterward reinforces my commitment to do it. I either walk around my big old house or hit the treadmill. Because I watch and listen to a classical music lecture series as I walk on the treadmill, two things happen: First, as I said before, the time flies by because I am focused on the lecture and the music. Second, I'm getting a double bang for my buck because I'm getting the exercise I need for my health, combined with filling my noggin with a learning experience. So, I'm not doing something that I hate (exercising); I'm listening to a great lecture and listening to beautiful music, while walking at a brisk clip. If you prefer to exercise outside by walking or jogging, use an audiotape for the same purpose. If you just like to walk or jog and take in the scenery, that's great too.

Because exercise is so important, and the lack of it impacts your relationship with time, I suggest that you *think of exercise as a time-gnat* that needs to be killed. Kill it by writing it down and immediately removing it from your Dead Gnat File, and then put it into your calendar as a regularly scheduled appointment. Don't forget to load the tape or CD.

Driving: Create Time

If your business requires lengthy car trips, you have an opportunity to create time. Audio books and lectures on countless topics are available for purchase or loan from your local library. I don't intend to be too preachy here. If you relish the opportunity to listen to music, the news, or talk radio, please do so. But I point out that there is an opportunity here to create educational time for yourself while performing a necessary function—driving. It's your call.

Synchronous or Asynchronous Communication: Create Time

In his wonderful book on modern technology, *Being Digital,* Nicholas Negroponte made a point that has stuck with me ever since I read it in 1996: there is a difference between synchronous and asynchronous communication. Synchronous communication is any kind of communication that goes on with *all parties present,* whether it's during a phone call or an in-person meeting. You ask a question, you get an answer; you make a point, the other person counters it; you make a suggestion, and the other person or people weigh in on it right away. Synchronous communication is great and necessary when stuff needs to go back and forth for immediate resolution. Asynchronous communication, on the other hand, is any communication that doesn't require the presence of other people. You have an appointment to meet with Joe next Tuesday at 11 and suddenly realize you need to change it. You can call Joe (synchronous communication) or send an e-mail or text message (asynchronous communication), saying, "Joe, next Tuesday doesn't work. How about the same time on Wednesday or Thursday?" We do this all the time, or do we? What Negroponte suggested, and what I am suggesting to you, is that we quickly make decisions on what needs to be synchronous and what doesn't need immediate resolution. For simple questions or simple answers, the telephone can be a gigantic time waster. First you call and go to the person's voicemail, where you leave a message. Then the person gets back to you, only to go to *your* voicemail, and you both are suddenly engaged in the modern game of phone tag. E-mail or text messaging solves this problem when the thing being communicated is simple and requires only an answer or an alternative. I assume that the vast majority of people reading this book use e-mail or know how to send a text message. What I am suggesting here is that you *create time* by always asking yourself if what you are about to communicate needs to be synchronous, requiring the presence of others, or whether it could be asynchronous. I cannot give you a list of issues that require two people to communicate back and forth, and neither can you. It's a judgment call you make throughout the day. But consider that the more you can communicate without the need of the other person's presence, the more time you will create.

Your Paper Organizer or Your PDA—or Both

APT Alert: This is the perfect blend of practice and technology. Nothing—NOTHING—has a greater impact on your time than a well-maintained appointment calendar combined with your to-do list. Screw up your calendar, and you waste time showing up for appointments at the wrong time. Neglect your to-do list, and you spend your day creating time-gnats. I won't belabor this because I believe that it is self-evident that you need to keep an orderly calendar and list of things to do.

But what should you use, a paper organizer such as a Day-Timer or a PDA (Personal Digital Assistant)? A few years ago, you would carry a PDA and a cell phone. Now, the two have been combined into the smartphone. We are all fixed in our ways, and over time, we tend to do things that have worked for us in the past. Simply said, we develop useful habits. This is not a bad thing! Some people, me included, have become so accustomed to their Day-Timers that to abandon it puts a torpedo through our familiar way of doing things. Stop beating yourself up and thinking that you're a Luddite just because you are accustomed to an old fashioned paper-based calendar and list system. Some habits are good, and just because you are in the habit of writing stuff down and crossing things off, you are not crazy.

Like most people, however, I have long recognized that technology has created useful new ways of keeping me organized. PDAs are wonderful instruments and are now almost universally combined with a cell phone into what we call a smartphone. In one little device, such as my Blackberry or an iPhone, you have a telephone, a camera, a calendar, a to-do list, pictures of your kids and grandkids, and the Internet, including e-mail. If you're waiting in a line, you can read the news, check your portfolio or, if you're really bored, play a game. I synchronize my Outlook calendar, to-do list, and contact list between my desktop computer and my Blackberry. Your office is in your pocket! In the "old days" (not too long ago), if you were on the road and realized you had to call someone, you would pull to the side of the road, find a phone booth that, with any luck, had a phone book, look up the number, feed coins into the phone, and make the call. Talk about wasting time! The smartphone has revolutionized that mess, and as voice recognition software constantly improves, it's only going to get better. And it's quite good now. Pick up your smartphone and say "call Pete Miller." It beats looking up a phone number. Yes, the smartphone is here to stay.

But what about people, especially Baby Boomers like me, who have been raised on paper organizers? A few years ago I received a Palm Pilot PDA as a gift. It wasn't a phone, but as an organizer I loved it, for a while. I didn't renew my annual subscription to my beloved Day-Timer because I was now a digital guy. Not for long. I gradually realized that my years of reliance on my Day-Timer had become habit forming—good habits. I missed the physical satisfaction of scribbling down an idea, or checking off an item completed, or crossing off an unnecessary task. When someone told me something important, I would simply jot it down. The Palm Pilot had an interesting feature called Graffiti, which was a sort of stenographic language that enabled you to scribble words right on the screen. I never mastered it, and found that it was taking me so long I was getting frustrated. It wasn't saving time; it was wasting it. Users of popular smartphones use their thumbs to type in stuff. I hate it. A bad, but true, pun is that Baby Boomers are all thumbs. I finally relented and ordered a new set of Day-Timer monthly books. Did this mean that I was going backward, ignoring the amazing technology of the PDA? No. I came up with a simple but revolutionary idea that I now share with you.

A Radical Idea – PaperPlus – Use both your paper organizer and your smartphone

I hear what you're saying. Hey, Moran, first you talk about creating or manufacturing time, and now you're suggesting that we get redundant—and use more time! This is contradictory! No, it isn't. What I am recommending is a new Best Practice, one that I think you should start immediately. EXCEPTION: If you are comfortable with thumbing stuff into your smartphone and consider paper a bother, do not change what you are doing. Just as Boomers were raised on paper, X-Gens, Y-Gens, and Millennials have been raised on digital devices. As paper is natural to some people, a digital device is natural to others. Note: I use the word *natural*. If you try to adopt a practice that isn't natural to you, frustration awaits. For those of you who don't like or need a paper organizer, my only advice is to do regular hand exercises to avoid future arthritis. I'm serious. For those of you who are wedded to your paper organizer but recognize the obvious benefits of digital devices, let's look at my PaperPlus proposal and see how it works.

Put your to-do or task list into your paper organizer. You can add things while you're having breakfast in a diner without spilling coffee on your Blackberry. As you complete tasks, perform your old familiar procedure by checking it off or crossing it out. Also, put appointments into the calendar section. If you get new contact information from someone, put that down in the notes section. Have an idea? Put it down as a note.

Every day—*EVERY DAY*—set time aside to transcribe what you put into your paper organizer into your computer. Note: this assumes that you synchronize the information in your computer with your smartphone. Unless you are a two-finger typist, this transcription process should take only a few minutes. Here's what happens with the PaperPlus practice: while you are adding an additional chore to your day, you are beginning a Best Practice that so many people ignore; you are *reviewing what happened,* which causes you to prioritize stuff as your review it. Some things are trivial and should not be transcribed, like errands such as "pick up milk." Some things are very important and will continue to be so: "Call accountant about audit."

Using PaperPlus, you are empowering your good old habit of jotting stuff down but, by transcribing the important information, you are doing something you could not do with your paper organizer: you are creating a searchable database of information that you may need to access in the future. In the mid-1980s, I took a course in the proper use of a Day-Timer, and the speaker suggested putting paper clips on pages that contained important information that you may need to retrieve. Lame! Before I started using a PDA and the PaperPlus approach, I would spend hours looking up some item that I needed to verify. I use the pocket, coat-sized Day-Timer. Each month is a separate booklet, which gets filed in a box at the end of the month. It's a great system, but NOT for retrieving archival information. Digital totally trumps paper here. So, you are creating time by using PaperPlus, not wasting it. You save hours by not having to look up an item on paper. But, most important, you are adopting a killer Best Practice. Review your day, every day. It is time well invested.

Chapter 8 Summary

In this chapter I discussed the following:

- The meaning of time
- Manufacturing time by changing your perception.
- Time-gnats and how to kill them
- Allowing your desk to clean itself
- Create more time by getting in shape
- Driving creates time
- Synchronous and asynchronous communication
- Your paper organizer or your PDA, or both
- PaperPlus gives you the best of both worlds

CHAPTER 9

Finance

APT Principles: Practice, with a bit of Attitude and Technology

You can delegate a lot of things. You have to. But when it comes to the financial aspects of your business, even though you delegate, you must be on top of it like white on rice. You and I have heard stories over the years or have read about them in the newspaper about a business tanking because a subordinate, through negligence, stupidity, or criminal intent, played havoc with the finances of a business or organization.

In this chapter, I focus on the key parts of your company's finances, asking you to use the *APT Principle,* not only to avoid trouble, but to make financial controls your ally and not something left to others. Your degree of involvement obviously depends on the size of your business. In a very small business, it might mean checking the numbers once a week and conferring with your bookkeeper. In larger organizations, it might mean regular meetings with a financial vice president or controller. But small or large, the point is the same: finances require your active attention. This is a Best Practice.

Budgeting

Whether as CEO of my own company or as a member of a not-for-profit board, I always thought of a budget like the rails on a ship or boat. Most of the time, the rail is just there, doing nothing. But in times of turbulence, rails keep you from falling overboard. Budgeting is not something that shows up naturally; you must force yourself to budget. It should be done toward the end of the year for the following year, or right now if you don't have one. If it's only you and a bookkeeper, forget the bookkeeper. *You* do the budget. You may confer with the bookkeeper once you've drafted the budget, but recognize that this is a management job.

Budgeting Requires a LOT of Thought

Budgeting takes time, but it's not terribly difficult, especially if you have good financial statements to work with. Use software such as Intuit's QuickBooks or Quicken if you have a fairly simple operation, or full-blown accounting software if your enterprise is large. The first step is to simply line up all of the chart-of-account lines from a prior year, and then fill in the anticipated numbers for the year ahead. This is simple, conceptually, but it takes thought—a lot of it. Simply slapping on an increase percentage formula isn't budgeting. You must examine each line, getting input from your employees. You can't think of everything, and employee input is vital. You may think it's okay to plug in the same number as last year for copier costs, but when an employee points out that the copier has been acting up and getting worse by the day, you need to make note of it. Remember, I'm talking about the first draft here; someone needs to research a new copier and its costs. Because the business has grown, you might discover that you need a much bigger copier with lots more features, and that all this will add a few thousand more to the budget for next year. Better to discover that now than to create a budget gap that will show up mid-year because you didn't anticipate the new costs. Many budget entries require quite a bit of research before you can plug in a realistic number. Insurance is a big one. Contact your broker to see if market conditions or increased risks will raise your premiums next year. I just read that the average health insurance policy is increasing nine percent. You might need a soothsayer to figure out how to budget your health insurance premiums, but always put in a large increase for this budget line! For every single line entry, ask yourself, "Is there any reason this should change, up or down, next year?" Be rigorous.

WK – "Who Knows?" – A Key Expense Budget Line

You may call it "unanticipated expenses," which is exactly what the line means, but always plug something like this into your expense budget. Make it a healthy figure. It helps to have a line like this when something out of the blue happens to another line in your budget. This is where you get the numbers to keep the budget on track. If you were diligent in anticipating expenses, the WK line should come in at the end of the year with a lot of money left there. I know a guy who has a car-towing business. On the front of his truck is the inscription: "Shit Happens." It does.

Income: Budget and Business Plan Distinguished

On the income side of the budget, I recommend using caution. This is a budget, not a business plan, and if your business plan has exciting (but realistic) sales projections, good budgeting demands that you be conservative. By all means, work your business plan and shoot for the big numbers; just don't budget that way. Think hard, and ask a lot of people a lot of questions about your anticipated revenue. Knowledge of your market and existing customer base is crucial. The stability of a revenue stream can be severely upset by an unanticipated problem in your customer base. My old company did a lot of business with state and local governments. Over the years, when tax revenues took a hit because of the economy, our top and bottom line took a hit as well. *APT Alert: Practice.* Make sure your business plan addresses any problems of too much market concentration. In the wicked winter of 2011, businesses in the Midwest saw their budgets challenged because of the constant snow and ice storms. Conservative revenue figures in your budget will smooth out jolts to your income.

Purchasing

First, you'll want to buy green eyeshades, the classic icon of the penny-wise manager. Frugal purchasing is especially important when things are humming along nicely, revenue and profits are up, and cash flow is good. It's easy to be lax here because there's plenty of money in the bank, and there doesn't appear to be any reason to skimp. This is the time to bargain, and if you're in good financial shape, bargaining is easier. You can take advantage of cash discounts, early payment breaks, and volume purchase discounts.

Be very careful about delegating when it comes to purchasing. I once had an enthusiastic marketing director who bought $3,500 worth of pens with the company name on them. That was 14 years ago. I still have boxes of them, and because my company was sold and changed its name, they are worthless, except as pens. Depending on the size of your operation, some business owners require all invoices to be approved by the boss. This isn't a bad idea. At the minimum, I recommend that you review expense reports regularly, even if you don't pre-approve all invoices, and ask lots of questions of your accounts payable person or people. This lets them know that you're watching.

Not only should you focus on what is being bought, but you should know how it is paid for. I once had a bookkeeper, a very pleasant and ethical woman, who thought that the right thing to do was to pay an invoice within a week of receiving it, even if it required payment in 30 days. Think about this. For every bill that is paid before it is due, you would need a corresponding increase in your revenue to offset the negative change in cash flow. I taped a sign on her computer screen: "Pay no bill before it's due." I made exceptions for local contractors; they got paid within days, if not immediately. When we needed a carpenter, plumber, or electrician, I wanted them to know that my company was a ready source of income. Make nice with people who you may need NOW.

But 30 days is the norm for most businesses. It's crazy to shorten the time for payment.

Cash and Investments

Having good cash flow and a lot of money in an account is the place you want to be. If you have a sudden and necessary expense, it saves you from having to pay interest on a credit line. As your cash mounts, you need to huddle with a financial counselor to see how it should be invested. Your counselor will always say conservatively, because the cash may be needed; but if it's a lot of cash, investing part of the amount in equities—which can fluctuate a lot—is often a good idea. The typical cash barrel for a small company is a money market fund—highly liquid and safe. Good cash management dictates that you make regular contributions to the money market fund. For good reason, we are reluctant to touch funds in an interest-bearing account, even if the interest is modest. This reluctance is positive; it helps the fund to grow. Over time it makes the balance sheet look great, which makes bankers smile. Well, maybe not smile, but frown less.

A note on sales tax: Depending on your business and whether you must collect sales tax at all, this can be a meaningless burden. I say meaningless because you only shoulder the administrative burden of preparing the sales tax return, monthly or quarterly, depending on your state and its regulations. The important thing to recognize is that sales tax receipts are NOT YOUR MONEY. You merely collect it from your customers and pass it along to the taxing entity when required. I knew a guy who looked at sales tax as a quarterly nightmare. He would put all of his receipts into one bank account, and when sales tax was due, he faced a huge payment, and it always seemed like a surprise. Obviously, his cash flow was poor. But whether your cash flow is a torrent or a trickle, the Best Practice is to set aside a part of every deposit an amount equal to the percent that is the sales tax into a separate account, preferably interest bearing. Just do it. When sales tax is due, it is a simple procedure of paying it out of the separate account. If your weekly gross receipts are $15,000, your quarterly receipts are $180,000. In Suffolk County, New York, for example, your sales tax liability would be 8.625 percent of $180,000 or $15,525. If you set aside the amount daily (assuming a five-day week) with each deposit, you would pay to the separate account each day $259—hardly noticeable. This is a simple application of the old "Christmas Club" or layaway account, where you make many small deposits and then have a lot to spend when you need it. Collecting and paying sales tax should be nothing more than a pain in the ass, not a nightmare.

A thriving business should have a balanced investment portfolio, just like an individual. And just as with the individual investor, a common stock portfolio should not be made up of funds that need to be accessed fast, but should instead be considered a long-term investment.

Financial Statements: Audit, Review, or Compilation

What kind of financial statements should your accountant prepare for you? An audit is the highest form of a financial statement. It is a long and cumbersome operation, and it also costs a lot of money. Accountants charge a lot for an audit, understandably, because they don't write on the report that they are just relying on what you told them; rather, they have audited the company, and they stand behind the numbers. Auditing is like picking the fly crap out of the pepper. It takes time. Usually, it's unnecessary to have an audit done every year unless you are gearing up to sell your business. Even then, wait to get into the deal, and then negotiate over the cost of an audit if the purchaser wants one. I discuss selling your business in detail in the final chapter.

A compilation is the lowest and cheapest of financial statements that an accountant prepares. On the statement are words from the accountant that basically says the accountant hasn't the foggiest idea if what you told him or her is correct, but for whatever it's worth, here are the numbers. *APT Alert: Practice.* I recommend the middle ground for *most* companies: the *review* financial statement. Although a review is less complicated and extensive than an audit, it is more extensive than a compilation, and it does provide a basis for the accountant to express a limited assurance that the accountant did not become aware of any material changes that should be made to the financial statements. Essentially, a review is designed to enable an accountant, without applying comprehensive audit procedures, to assess management's representations and to consider whether the financial statement appears to conform to generally accepted accounting principles (GAAP).

Electronic Banking

Anything that saves time and money makes me smile, and it should make you smile, too. This discussion could easily have fit in the time-management chapter. If you don't already, I strongly recommend that you inquire into using electronic banking, if only for your payables. This is especially so for regular and recurring monthly payments that don't change, such as lease payments. Without any human intervention, the payment automatically goes out on a given date. This is a big time saver. Even with payments that vary, the bookkeeper simply calls up the blank check on the computer screen, starts typing, and the vendor information populates the check. Just put in the invoice number, the amount of the check, and any notes in the memo field, and then click enter.

Your company's finances are critical to the success of your business. Remember, it is the job of senior management to keep on top of the numbers.

Chapter 9 Summary

In this chapter, I discussed the following:

- Budgeting
- A key expense budget line
- Budget distinguished from business plan
- Purchasing
- Cash and investments
- Financial statements (audit, review, or compilation)
- Electronic banking

CHAPTER 10

Marketing Your Business and Creating Your Brand

APT Principles: Attitude, Practices, and a bit of Technology

Marketing is Telling People What You Do—Over, and Over, and Over

I don't know where I heard or read the above saying, but it is the best definition of marketing I have ever encountered. Never think of marketing as a project or series of projects that you get around to periodically. You need to shift your **attitude** to think of marketing as you think of breathing: you don't think about it; you just do it. Of course there are marketing projects, involving detailed planning, execution, and assessment. Projects involve long meetings, careful record keeping, and constant revision. Your formal marketing plan is a critical part of your business plan, but I am talking about the everyday marketing that you don't plan for and, like breathing, you just do it. Marketing can be the way you handle an irate customer, or it can be the way you ask a happy customer for a referral or a testimonial. Marketing can be a chat with a stranger in an elevator. (I will discuss your Elevator Talk later.) Marketing can be a letter to the editor, a charitable contribution, a kind word for a potential customer, or attending meetings of various organizations. It is telling people what you do—over and over and over.

Branding

The American Marketing Association (AMA) defines a brand as a "name, term, sign, symbol, or design, or a combination of them intended to identify the goods and services of one seller or group of sellers and to differentiate them from those of other sellers." Branding has been the buzz in marketing for many years. To the extent that you can distinguish yourself in the marketplace, you begin to become a household name. Establishing your brand and getting the word out—over and over and over—is a Best Practice. Microsoft performed this feat brilliantly starting in the early 1980s. With a simple, brilliant name—*Microsoft*—the company established its brand in the eyes of the consumer as the people who created *software* for *microcomputers*. It didn't stop there. *Word* has become a synonym for word processing in the eyes of many, or most, consumers. *Windows* used to be things that you would look through and wash occasionally.

Marketing and Sales: What's the Difference?

Marketing is everything that you do to reach and persuade prospective customers or clients, by telling them what you do (over and over and over). Good marketing establishes your brand. Sales are everything that you do to close the sale, or get your customer to make the purchase. Both marketing and sales are necessary to the success of a business.

If you don't do any marketing today, tomorrow won't look very different, nor will the next day. But if you don't do any marketing today, a year from now, things will look very different, and it will not look pretty. Real estate developers cultivate a knack for patience because the things they do today won't bear fruit for a long time, often many years. There is site selection, surveying, possible demolition, constant meetings with architects and engineers. There are also meetings with lawyers and accountants, all of whom are deeply involved in dealing with city hall and the ongoing permit process. Patience. When they cut the ribbon on a newly finished project, all of that long-ago flurry of activity is suddenly justified, and as the first units are sold or the new tenants start to move in, the developer is happy he or she spent the time years before. We should all borrow a page from real estate developers and cultivate that patience, knowing that our efforts today will eventually be paid off at a distant tomorrow, and this is especially so with marketing. Marketing is not something to be put off.

In this and the next two chapters, I will discuss the basics, some of which you never thought had anything to do with marketing.

Don't let your business be the world's best kept secret. You can have the best product or service on the planet, but if nobody knows about it, you might as well not have it at all. We all hear about those quaint stories about somebody who became a raving success just on word of mouth alone. "I don't spend a nickel on marketing; my customers just bring me the new customers." Well, fine, but there are two problems with this story. First, I don't believe it; second, if success came from word-of-mouth alone, how much more successful that person would have been with some marketing efforts. Don't get me wrong. Word of mouth is excellent, and it is a form of marketing in itself, but customer referrals alone will not make a business. I might make an exception here for a specialist, such as a skilled cabinet maker. The decision might not be to expand and deal with employee problems, but to earn good money from his well-honed skills alone. Word of mouth may be just the ticket for such an individual. But even the skilled cabinet maker would agree: he is the exception, not the rule.

Marketing is not just about getting new customers, a mistake many people make. Marketing means taking care of your existing customers, including such simple things as keeping in touch or letting your customers know when you have come out with a new product or service. In the early days of Intuit, makers of the category-killing financial software solutions Quicken and QuickBooks, they got most things right, except for marketing to existing customers. I was an early Quicken adopter, and I loved it from the start. But, crazy as this may sound, Intuit, in the old days (back in the 1980s), did not notify existing customers when a new release came out, relying instead on their regular advertising. They soon got their act together, perhaps in response to ranting letters from me. I was so happy with the software that I would immediately order the next version just upon notification. Sell first to the people who already like you and use your products or services.

Marketing is not the sole province of management or the sales team. Every employee in the organization has to be aware of the importance of telling people about the business. Your employees' future depends on it, so why not let them know they are part of the marketing team? Your employees are a big part of your marketing efforts, both with existing customers and new ones.

The Elevator Talk: Ground Zero for Your Marketing

I don't know who coined the phrase "elevator talk" or "elevator speech," but it is a simple yet brilliant concept. The idea is that you meet someone while getting onto an elevator on a high floor. You engage each other in conversation, and you are asked the question, "What do you do?" You have a minute or so before the car reaches the first floor, so what you say in response has to be compelling and leave the other person wanting to know more. Have you ever heard someone say, "I don't memorize what I'm going to say because I don't want it to sound canned." Nonsense! Jot this down: the more you memorize a speech, the less canned it will sound. The words are firmly embedded in your head, freeing you to act natural and answer questions. Your elevator talk should be just that, a talk, not a simple recitation of your business card. I take exception with most opinions of what an elevator talk should be. In my view, an elevator talk *needs to lead to a question,* from the listener to you. I suggest *Moran's Rule of Elevator Talk:* if your elevator talk does not result in a question, it's not worth giving the talk. Let's look at a few examples, all of which answer the question, "What do you do?" and all of which result in a question:

Bad: "I sell old auto parts."

Better: "I prevent people who work on old cars from going insane."

Bad: "I'm a financial planner."

Better: "I specialize in Austrian Economics." A guy hit me with this once, and I was so curious I had to keep asking questions. "How does that work?" I asked. So the guy responds, "I use the principles of Austrian economist Friedrich Hayek and show people how to secure financial freedom without government calling the shots." Wow.

Bad: "I'm an intellectual property lawyer."

Better: "I help people to capitalize on what they produce."

Bad: "I'm an accountant."

Better: "I run numbers and make people happy with the results." Yes, humor can be an excellent part of your elevator talk.

Bad: "I'm an insurance broker."

Better: "I make the future less scary."

You get the idea. The objective of an elevator talk is to say something *interesting* that makes the other person want to ask questions. I have heard some opinions that elevator talks should encapsulate what you do in two or three sentences. I humbly disagree. How does this sound as elevator talk for an insurance agent: "I help people preserve their assets, avoid calamity, and secure their future by making the future more predictable; and I use various products to do that." Yada, yada, yada. Yakitty, yakitty, yak. You lost me at the word *assets*. It makes me want to pry open the elevator doors and jump off. I prefer a simple and punchy phrase with the *sole objective to solicit a question from the listener*. Then, you will be answering the listener's questions, and people who ask questions usually listen to the answers.

Practice your elevator talk with your spouse, your friends and colleagues, and even your kids. Don't forget to talk to the mirror. Soon, elevators will become your favorite form of transportation.

In the next two chapters, we're going to drill down further into the wonderful world of marketing.

Chapter 10 Summary

In this chapter, I discussed the following:

- Marketing: telling people what you do, over and over and over
- Branding
- Marketing versus sales
- Market to existing customers, not just new ones
- Your elevator talk

CHAPTER 11

Public Speaking, a Branding Opportunity

APT Principles: Attitude and Practices

It doesn't matter what kind of organization you run, there are times when you will need to speak in public, and I'm not talking about elevator speeches. Some view this as an excellent marketing opportunity, whether the subject is your business specifically or your industry and its effects on the audience. Make no mistake about it: it is a great opportunity. Do a good job and you will be asked to speak in front of other groups. Organizations of all types are on the constant look-out for speakers, and landing a speaking engagement is quite easy. All you need do is send a notice of your availability to as many groups as you can identify. Rotary clubs, for example, meet weekly, usually for lunch. Every club has a program chairperson whose job you can make easier by volunteering to give a talk. Say, for example, you head an insurance agency. Hurricane season (June to November) is a great time to speak to people about disaster preparedness. You give a good talk, providing real value for the audiences and, of course, you leave behind literature with your name and company contacts. The deal is simple. You provide value by giving an informative talk, and in return you have the opportunity to introduce yourself to prospective customers. This is marketing at its best: person-to-person contact with real people.

It's important to keep in mind that your speaking engagement should not be a simple sales pitch. Nothing turns off an audience more than being captive to somebody just hawking his wares. Your talk should be peppered with phrases such as "Whether you deal with my company or someone else's, you should always be aware of such and such." People expect subtle plugs, just not an infomercial. What I just said sounds easy, doesn't it? You contact a bunch of organizations that are already looking for speakers, and you land engagements that give you the opportunity to show your stuff. But I recognize that speaking in public appeals to some people as much as sleeping with rattle snakes. Statistically, public speaking tops the list of things that people fear most, more so than even death. It even has a scary-sounding name: glossophobia. Jerry Seinfeld once quipped that most people would rather be the corpse than the one who delivers the eulogy. There is something about standing in front of a gathering of people that causes profound anxiety for some people. If you are one of those who are absolutely frightened by the idea of speaking in public, don't feel bad: you are not alone. Any curbside psychologist will tell you that your fear probably has something to do with a childhood memory, long suppressed. As a kid you may have once sounded out in public, only to be batted down by some adult, probably a parent, and you were made to feel ashamed and embarrassed. Your little brain got the message that speaking in public is a bad thing. Your hidden self now recalls that shame and embarrassment, and it shows up in your adult life as fear.

Fortunately, I had a very positive experience with my first talk in public. I was 13 years old, big for my age at

5'11", with a voice that had already "cracked," so I didn't sound very young. My teacher, Sister Carol Anton, asked me to give a speech at a graduation assembly on the subject of George Washington. She spent hours coaching me, teaching me the basics of eye contact, gestures, and speaking from the chest, not the throat. The day of the speech I was not frightened. I had no fear because I probably did not have an earlier negative experience in my childhood with public speaking; I had a wonderful and caring teacher who prepared me for the job. I was ready. Decades later I can still remember how my speech ended, "First in war, first in peace, first in the hearts of his countrymen." But after my speech came the real payoff. There were many adults present, and they, including Sister Carol Anton, praised me to the roof. How does that make a 13-year old feel? Great! I have been speaking in public ever since. I don't care if the audience is five people or five thousand, I'm good to go. I had a positive experience at a young and impressionable age, and it is still with me. Heights, on the other hand, scare the hell out of me. I don't recall the childhood experience, but it must have been a whopper. I'm not too crazy about snakes either. But speaking in public—no problem, thanks to Sister Carol Anton.

But you may not have had the positive experience that Sister Carol Anton gave me. You may fall into that large cohort of folks who fear the podium and go through life letting opportunities slip through their hands because of a long-forgotten childhood incident. Time for an **attitude** check. First, simply recognize that you have a fear of speaking in public. Yes, you have the fear, and don't deny it. We don't get to pick our phobias—they were picked for us.

How to Overcome Your Fear of Public Speaking

There is an old Zen proverb: "The first step to enlightenment is observation." So, I'm asking you to observe that you are afraid of the podium. But this does not mean that you should continue to avoid speaking in public or, for those times when you can't avoid it, experience the terrible anxiety and all that goes with it—the pounding chest, the soaking armpits, and the pain in your stomach. What you need to do is change your reality. There are a number of reality-changing organizations out there that are dedicated to helping you overcome your fear of public speaking. Just Google "public speaking fear," and you will find a small industry of folks dedicated to helping you solve the problem. The Dale Carnegie Course, the granddaddy of courses that help people speak in public, began almost 100 years ago in 1912, when Dale Carnegie himself began teaching his famous course at a YMCA. Definitely investigate www.dalecarnegie.com. Toastmasters International, founded in 1942, is another venerable organization that helps people learn to speak in public. See www.toastmasters.org. Other organizations you can turn to include fearlesspresentations.com, speakingwithoutfear.com, stresscure.com (this site has a very good paper on the subject), mypublicspeakingfear. org, nosweatspeaking.com, and countless others. Help is out there. It's up to you to reach out. I would love to introduce you when you give your next talk.

The Four Categories of Public Speakers

1. **The Fearful**. You are *dreadfully afraid* of public speaking. I discussed this above: you need help, and it's out there. Go get it.

2. **The Uncomfortable**. You are *uncomfortable* with public speaking, with some fear perhaps, but you just don't like to speak in public, and you do so reluctantly.

3. **The Terrible**. You are not at all afraid of speaking in public and do so often, but you *are terrible,* and you don't notice that your audience begins to slip away, or falls asleep. You don't prepare because you don't care. You just like to mouth off. There are a lot of you out there. Your job is to get better, to deliver value to your audience, or please, just shut up.

4. **The Good.** You are a good public speaker, perhaps a great one.

Tips and Tools for Public Speaking

The following are time-honored tips, and they are aimed at categories 2, 3, and 4 above. As for category 1, reading these tips won't help you; get some training instead.

Prepare, prepare, prepare. For me, this is the most important principle. Over the years, when I ran my legal publishing and research company, I would often be invited to speak before bar associations, which were fabulous opportunities because I was speaking directly to my market. I would typically spend at least *one full day* preparing my talk. I would print out my notes in large type, so I could see where I was at a glance (they never supplied teleprompters). I would walk around my office and deliver my speech, sometimes going home to avoid distractions. I would then deliver it to my wife and sometimes to some of my staff. I even delivered it to Molly, my Golden Retriever, who, needless to say, was enraptured. The last thing I wanted my clients to see was a guy who stumbled around from one topic to another in a disjointed stream of consciousness. Not only would it hurt my brand, but it would ensure that I would never be invited back again. I was locked and loaded, and I was always invited back. My command of my material gave me tremendous confidence because I knew that I would entertain the audience and could answer any question that came up. Preparation rules the day. I knew a guy who loved to speak in public and would seize any opportunity to do so. He clearly fell into category 3; he was *terrible,* an insufferable bore who never got to the point because it wasn't apparent he had one to get to. But he was a great guy and raised a lot of money for charity— although not because of his public speaking. His talks were rambling, unprepared, unfocused bits of information that popped into his head. Because we belonged to many of the same local organizations, I would often encounter him as a speaker, and whenever I did, I would sit near the door and fake my Blackberry buzzing and hurry out at an appropriate moment. He had no fear of speaking, but audiences feared *him.* He showed an absolute lack of preparation. Deliver to your audience, and you will be invited back.

Move. If your material is complicated and you need to be at the podium to refer to your notes, that's perfectly okay, but by all means move—your head, your shoulders, your hands. It helps keep the audience focused. **Practice gestures,** and use them at appropriate times.

Speak from your diaphragm, not your throat. This is speech class 101. The diaphragm is the large muscle that separates the chest or thoracic cavity from the abdomen. People who have learned to speak from the diaphragm, rather than the throat, know that it gives resonance and authority to your voice. Compare Gilbert Gottfried, the very funny but whiney comedian to President Obama. Gottfried is pure throat, which he uses to comedic effect. President Obama, on the other hand, is a master of diaphragmatic speaking. His voice can resonate through a stadium or a meeting room. I leave it to you to judge the content of his speeches, but his delivery is flawless. It takes practice; it can be mastered.

Include the room in your view, looking to different parts of the audience. Some people get nervous making eye contact with an individual in the audience. If this is you, look to distant parts of the audience rather than the closer attendees. If you look to the back of the room, as some speaking coaches suggest, do not look up at the ceiling, but just over the heads of the people in the last row. Looking someone square in the eye is difficult for a long period of time. Actors are coached to look at their fellow actor's nose or cheekbone, not the eyes, in a scene that requires a face-to-face encounter. If you look someone straight in the eye, you might notice a pained expression. What you don't know is that the person with the pained look on his face just remembered that he forgot an important appointment, and the look on his face had nothing to do with your talk.

Get out of your head. I knew a political leader who was a terrific speaker when addressing his team of committee people or other party officials. You felt like he was talking to you. He was relaxed, genuine, made easy jokes, and strong points. But whenever he spoke in front of a large public gathering, he turned into a wooden statue. In front of his political team, he concentrated on his message and what he wanted to communicate. At public gatherings, he crawled right into his head and was concerned about how he was coming across, rather than on what he wanted to put across. It's not about you; it's about your message. *Concentrate on your message,* and you will look good; concentrate on how you look, and you will look uncomfortable.

The audience is not out to get you. Think of yourself when you are a member of the audience. Are you waiting for the speaker to slip up, hoping that it happens? Of course not; you want the speaker to be good, effective, and to not waste your time. You are on the speaker's side: you both want the same thing—a good, informative talk. The same holds when you are on the other side of the podium. Even after many years of public speaking, I realize that I have a hard time with a *pickle puss,* someone with a lousy expression on his face, which may show up as boredom, anger or, worst of all, contempt. Pardon me while I climb out of my head. I also have realized, over the years, that many of these pickle pusses really just have a pickle for a puss, and it has nothing to do with their attitude toward me. I spoke at a book signing recently for one of my books, and there was one guy who I expected to throw up because he wore such an unpleasant face. After my talk, while I was signing the books, he came to me, slapped me on the shoulder, and loudly praised my talk. He then bought two books, one for him and one for his wife. A sweet pickle.

Small details can make a big difference. Some things seem obvious, but are nevertheless worth mentioning. If you are going to use audiovisual aids like a computer projector, make sure the damn thing works before you start your talk! Get there early to check it out. Arriving early is also a good idea just to give you a feel for the room. If the sun streams in from one side, make sure to speak from the other side so that the audience will not be squinting at a talking shadow. If you have materials to hand out, either pass them out yourself before the people arrive, or enlist the aid of someone in the organization to help you.

Handling jerks. I have a short fuse when people ask stupid questions, and I always try to remember this shortcoming of mine because I am in danger of violating the First Rule of Jerk Handling: *do not empower the jerk.* There is no hard and fast set of rules because hecklers heckle in many different ways, but remember this: the other people in the audience don't like jerks either, and you will notice some raised eyes or shaking heads as the performance artist does his or her thing. Try to enlist the aid of these allies by asking questions directed at them; they want to help you because they are embarrassed by the amateur comedian in their organization.

Public speaking is something you can't avoid, so it is best not to try. Learn to love it, or at least be neutral toward it.

Chapter 11 Summary

In this chapter I discussed the following:

- Public speaking as a branding opportunity
- How to overcome your fear
- Rating yourself as a public speaker
- Tips for public speaking
- The audience is on your side
- Small details make a difference
- How to handle jerks

CHAPTER 12

Writing and Recording Your Brand

APT Principle: Practice

Your name, or the name of your business, should be in front of people all of the time, and the more it is, the stronger your brand. I am not talking about advertising, which is important and is covered elsewhere, but rather seizing the opportunity to go public and letting your message be heard consistently. If you don't like to write, or you honestly believe that writing is not your best skill, consider assigning this task to a competent employee or hiring one of the thousands of freelance writers out there. Getting your name in print should be a basic component of your marketing plan. Writing establishes you and your company as *authoritative,* a key branding attribute. The more people see you in print, the more likely you are to form an element of trust, that you are the person or organization that is on top of the game. Caution: do not use every writing opportunity as a way to sell; your objective is to establish yourself as the go-to source. I once wrote an article for the Op-Ed page of *The New York Times* on jury verdict trends, the area that I and my company were known for. It was the best single piece of advertising that I ever did —and I got paid for it! Below, I review some of the writing possibilities that you can use to get the word out about you and your company.

Writing a Book

Writing a book is no easy task—trust me. But some people write a book not caring if they sell one copy; instead they write to *brand* themselves as being an authority on a subject. I have a friend, Dave Mansfield, who has a narrow specialty in the law—traffic violations. Most lawyers know little on the subject and shy away from it because the fees are too small to justify the time necessary. How do you cross examine a cop on a red light violation? Dave knows how. So, lawyers from miles around simply refer their traffic cases to Dave. He does quite well, handling a huge volume of business that other lawyers avoid. Dave tells me that the best marketing move he ever made was to take his knowledge of the subject and co-author a book about it, entitled *Defense of Speeding, Reckless Driving, and Vehicular Homicide*. The book is prominently placed behind Dave's desk, so that you can't look at him without seeing his book in the background. Would you not hire this guy if you just got your third speeding ticket and are about to lose your license? Of course you would—he wrote the book!

If you choose to write a book as part of your marketing plan, it is absolutely imperative that you write a *good* book. Nothing could be more self-defeating than to dash off some garbage, put a cover on it, and expect it to make you an authority. In the field of writing nonfiction, content is king.

The publishing industry is going through a revolution, and the sweeping changes benefit writers. Traditionally, to get a book published, you had to send out countless inquiry letters to publishers or literary agents. A few years ago, the only alternative to traditional publishing was a thing called *vanity publishing,* which required you to invest thousands of dollars to buy a roomful of books and then try to sell them yourself. Today, self-publishing has come into its own as a serious outlet for authors, especially first-time authors who don't have an entry ramp to traditional publishers. Remember, I am not discussing a book that you want to distribute for money, but one that will *establish your brand.* There is a growing list of companies that cater to people who want to publish their own book. These are often known as *one-off* presses. One-off means that you can print one book at a time. The incredible advances in printing technology means that you no longer have to print thousands of books in separate print runs. Besides printing your book, these companies offer a host of bundled packages that can include copy editing, exterior and interior design, marketing assistance, and listing your book with major book distributors. The prices vary from a few hundred dollars to a few thousand. Some of the major players in the field are AuthorHouse, iUniverse, Xlibris, CreateSpace, Lulu.com, and Outskirts Press. An excellent book on the subject of self-publishing companies is entitled *The Fine Print of Self-Publishing* by Mark Levine (Bascom Hill Publishing Group, 2011). The author reviews the major self-publishing companies, rates them, and provides a detailed explanation of their contracts and royalty structures. Most important, he suggests guidelines for you to follow depending on whether your objective is to sell books or just write a book for a limited market, such as your existing customers and prospective customers.

Letters to the Editor

If you read an article that involves your business or field of expertise, don't hesitate to fire off a letter to the editor and express your agreement or disagreement. Many newspapers, including *The New York Times,* will put brief biographical information at the end of your letter (assuming, of course, that it is accepted for publication). I read an article about former Supreme Court Justice Sandra Day O'Connor in which she criticized the popular election of judges, as opposed to appointing them. I had written extensively about this subject in my book *Justice in America,* so I fired off a letter to the editor of *The New York Times.* It was published in May 2010. Local papers especially are on the lookout for a well-written letter to the editor. If the paper publishes an online edition, and especially if it archives past information, your name will eventually bubble to the surface in search engines like Google or Bing.

Articles

A newspaper or magazine article in your name is an excellent *brand booster,* one that you will want to hang in your office or copy (with permission) and send to customers. Just as with a book, your article must be well-written and not overtly self-promotional; otherwise, it will never be accepted for publication. Don't overlook local magazines and newspapers, some of which will not even pay you. But you don't care if you get paid for the effort because your purpose is branding, not writing for money.

Newsletters

A company newsletter aimed at the public takes time and effort but can pay results beyond its cost. Some businesses—mortgage brokers spring to mind—use the services of a hired newsletter writing firm. The company designs and writes your newsletter, and it is printed with your logo and imprint. See, for example the GARP Newsletter Service, garponline.com. E-mail newsletters are becoming increasingly popular and cost very little to produce. Many organizations, especially not-for-profits, have switched their newsletters to strictly online versions because of the savings. Just make sure to have an "opt-out" link so that you don't run afoul of antispam laws.

Blog

Blog is shorthand for a *web log,* which is your own column that gives you the opportunity to express yourself whenever you want on any subject. It can be a website in itself or embedded as a separate part of a website. Most have an interactive feature, enabling viewers to post responses. There are blogs on countless subjects, from politics to fashion to cooking. On the Kindle alone, there are over thirteen thousand blogs listed for a subscription fee. The hit movie *Julie and Julia* was all about a young woman who created a 365-day blog about recipes from one of Julia Child's cookbooks. If you think that you can come up with a few things to say each week that concern your business or industry, you should consider a blog. It can be funny, controversial, or just plain serious—but it should be entertaining and make people want to come back for more. As time goes by, search engines will pick up the words in your blog entries. If you don't think that you can generate interesting content at least a few times a month, then you are just wasting your time. A blog site can be free; it depends on how many bells and whistles that you want to include. A site that many bloggers use is wordpress.com. There are ready-made templates to use, so you don't need to be a website designer to get started. You can have your own blog up and running in minutes. With the Internet swimming in blogs, don't expect yours to take off overnight. Actually, you might not care if it ever becomes a popular spot for people to visit. Your purpose, at a minimum, is to *further your brand* to your customers and prospective customers. You should have your blog's address on your business card and stationery. I think it's important to have your blog or website as part of your e-mail address because every time you send an e-mail, your site is there to be seen. Rather than your-name@gmail.com, isn't it more impactful to have your-name@yourwebsite or yourname@yourblogsite? This is a branding opportunity that most people seem to ignore. It should come up in your conversations, just like a good elevator talk, because it gives you another opportunity to establish yourself as a guru in your field. If you wish to see my blog, *The Moran Report—Politics, Business, Life*, visit www.morancom.com. My e-mail address is russ@morancom.com. Every time someone tells me they visited my blog, I always ask how they found out about it. The vast majority tell me that they noticed the website address on my e-mail address.

Social Media: Facebook, Twitter, and More

Social media sites, when boiled down to their essentials, are websites that enable users to share information with each other, and for those with whom you share information, to share that information with all of their contacts. Besides letting people know who had what for breakfast, social media sites played a major role in the rebellions across the Middle East and North Africa in 2011.

Facebook

Facebook is the monster of all social media websites. Founded in 2004, it has become a life-force worldwide with more than 600 million active users. By April 2010, it could boast that over 41 percent of the US population had a Facebook account. In January 2010, Goldman Sachs estimated the value of the company to be $50 billion, making Mark Zuckerberg, its founder, worth almost $7 billion. It began as a college project and quickly expanded into one of the greatest media movers and shakers in the world. Users create a personal profile, add other users as friends, and exchange messages, including automatic notifications when the users update their profile. Users can join common-interest user groups, organized by industry, profession, workplace, school, or any other categories. If privacy is your goal, Facebook is not for you. Its very idea is the opposite of privacy—but then, so is the very idea of marketing. Facebook is a medium for getting the word out. When was the last time you visited a Starbucks, Dunkin' Donuts, or McDonald's without seeing prominent signs asking you to visit their Facebook pages and "friend" them? Like it or not, Facebook is a part of life and an important part of business life. If you do not have a Facebook account, stop reading and set one up—NOW. I hate to be preachy, but Facebook is simply one of those things that you can't ignore. What I am writing here is not intended to be a primer on Facebook—they abound—but as an introduction and an encouragement for you to be a part of it. To follow somebody on Facebook, you "friend" them or become a fan. I recall a day when "friend" was a noun, but a phenomenon like Facebook commands its own language, so now *friend* is also a verb. If you are favorably impressed by an item that someone has posted on a Facebook page, you "like" it. You can also post a comment. When I first signed up with Facebook, I would never turn down a friend or fan recommendation from a mutual friend. It just seemed like simple politeness. I would get an e-mail message saying that "Bill Jones suggests you *friend* Peggy Sue" or whomever. I started to notice a proliferation of cookbook recipes, baby pictures, and inane comments from people I barely knew. I am much more cautious with accepting friend recommendations.

Twitter

Another social networking phenomenon is Twitter, launched in July 2006, it grew to over 175 million registered users in five years. Twitter is also referred to as a *microblogging* site, and the messages are micro indeed; they are limited to 140 characters. Some find this annoyingly limiting, but I find it a welcome challenge as a writer. Many people, understandably, couldn't see the importance of Twitter, and for years I was one of them.

We all heard the stories of people *tweeting* lovely little *bons mots* such as "Had scrambled eggs for breakfast, Dude," to which the typical response would be "LOL—BARF." But gradually Twitter came to be viewed as a valuable and succinct way of transmitting useful information. And to me, that is exactly what Twitter is good for: to send useful information to people who may be interested in what you have to say. A lot of the usefulness of Twitter is determined by those you "follow." I follow intelligent people, as I determine from their bio, as well as from the contents of their past tweets. A great way of gathering followers who may be interested in what you have to say is to see who is following the significant voices in your community of interest. Say you design specialized accounting software and want to reach the top accounting firms. You should see who follows the prominent voices in the profession by searching keywords, and then follow them. A large percentage of those you follow will "follow you back," and you are off to building a market segment. You build your prominence on Twitter by tweeting interesting and useful things, not just related to what you have to sell. Like many, I often tweet quotes from famous people that I think would be of interest to my followers. I recently tweeted a quote from the late economist Milton Friedman: "If you put the federal government in charge of the Sahara Desert, in five years there'd be a shortage of sand." A lot of people found that interesting and *retweeted* it to *their* followers. This is how a single tweet can go to tens of thousands of people within a minute.

When I am tweeting about something that is the subject of a newspaper article, I use a free software program called bit.ly.com to shorten a lengthy Internet link to fit within the 140- character limit. For example, I recently tweeted this: "Harlem Success Academy Charter School - 88% proficient in reading, 95% in math. 6 nearby pub schools? 31% and 39%." The link to the *Wall Street Journal* article is this: http://online.wsj.com/article/SB1 0001424052748703730804576312880501768962.html, which would bring me way beyond the 140-character limit. So, using bit.ly.com, I simply shortened the link to this: http://on.wsj.com/kVXhEw.

But how can you use Twitter to directly promote your business? Do it subtly. I often refer back to my own blog with a tweet like this: "The real estate meltdown. Who are the real victims? http://t.co/VstTKO7." Notice that I provide only a teaser; for readers to get the full idea, they have to click on the link, which brings them to my blog site. Once they are there, I have the opportunity to sell them one of my books. You might consider doing the same thing. Provide useful information in a tweet, and refer readers to your blog or website where you will educate them further and perhaps do business with them. Welcome to the new age of marketing, an age that didn't exist a few short years ago.

Writing about your business is unavoidable, and you should not want to avoid it. It is a basic component of creating your brand. I've said this before, but I'll repeat it here because it is so important. If you don't like to write or don't think you have the talent, there are scores of freelancers out there, some who specialize in busi-ness writing, who would love to have you as a client. Their fees are usually quite reasonable. How's this for a snappy piece of sports writing:"WISCONSIN appears to be in the driver's seat en route to a win, as it leads 51–10 after the third quarter. Wisconsin added to its lead when Russell Wilson found Jacob Pedersen for an eight-yard touchdown to make the score 44–3."

As with many sports reports, the article was written 60 seconds after the end of the game. So what? Why am I telling you this? Well, the article was written *by a computer*. Yes, computer-generated writing is coming soon. Narrative Science, a start-up company in Evanston, Illinois, is using artificial intelligence to generate articles. For an interesting description of this development, see Steve Lohr's "In Case You Wondered, a Real Human Wrote This Column" in *The New York Times,* September 10, 2011. As a writer, I think I hate this development. But, because I'm writing for you, I have to bring this to your attention. Full disclosure: I wrote this book myself. I used a computer, but the computer didn't write it. I will also write the next edition of this book. Maybe.

In the next chapter, I discuss whether you should use consultants and, if you do, how to use them.

Chapter 12 Summary

In this chapter I discussed the following:

- Writing: it's your brand, so record it
- Different writing venues as a part of your branding strategy
  - Books
  - Letters to the editor
  - Articles
  - Newsletters
  - Blog
  - Computer generated writing software

CHAPTER 13

Consultants

APT Principle: Practice

A lawyer, an accountant, and a consultant went deer hunting. All three spotted a deer about 100 feet ahead, and all fired at the same time. They then began arguing over who, actually, shot the deer. Out of the woods came their friend, the local game warden. He grabbed the deer by the antlers and looked at the wound. "The consultant got him," the warden announced. When they asked how he knew, he said, "It went in one ear and out the other."

People and companies spend fortunes on consultants, only to take the findings, put them in a drawer, and never look at them again. There seems to be a theory lurking in the world that if you hire a consultant, that act alone will do the trick. Of course, nobody actually formulates this thought but, in practice, it is what too often happens. The reason for this is simple: a good consultant will challenge the ordinary way that you do business, and this challenge may go deeply to the core of your beliefs. If you deeply cherish *your* way of doing things, do not hire a consultant.

A consultant exists for almost any imaginable area of human inquiry. From the high priced, world-class firms, such as McKinsey or Booz Allen Hamilton, to the guy who used to run a successful hot dog stand, there is a consultant for every need. I was once on a business trip in San Diego when I befriended a bunch of guys at the bar. "What do you guys do?" I asked. "We're SarBox Consultants," one of them proudly announced. A SarBox consultant is an expert in the Sarbanes–Oxley Act of 2002, named for sponsoring Senators Paul Sarbanes and Michael Oxley. The law is also known as the Public Company Accounting Reform and Investor Protection Act and was intended to set new disclosure and practice standards for U.S. public companies, boards, management, and accounting firms. The law was a response to some big public company investment scandals such as Enron and Tyco. Some people think that the purpose of the act was to drive public company executives and the accounting profession insane. With the passage of one single law, congress created a whole new breed of consultants to help businesses contend with it, and a vast new category of profit-eating costs.

The Right Consultant Can Do Wonders for Your Business

The reason for hiring a consultant is simple: you want somebody to show you how to make your business work better and become more profitable. That's it. If you hire a consultant for any other reason, you should probably start off with a psychotherapist. A consultant's job is to help you make your business better. Note that I say *help you.* After the consultant's assignment is done, it's up to you to implement the practices that he or she has recommended. Think of a consultant as a business doctor. Your doctor asks you questions about your health, diagnoses any problems, and then makes recommendations. Watch your diet, get more exercise, avoid this, eat more of that. These are the things the doctor will tell you, but it's up to you to carry them out. Some of the things the doctor tells you won't appeal to you because you will have to change the way you live your life and, in some cases, do without stuff that gives you pleasure and do things that you really would not like to do. It is not the doctor's job to make you feel happy, but to level with you on your health. And just like the doctor, the consultant is going to recommend some difficult courses of action, some new practices to put into motion, and other practices to drop.

We use consultants because we're too close to the business to get a clear view of what must be done. Another reason we hire consultants is to plug in specialized knowledge that you or your staff lacks. You can spend whatever leisure time you have boning up on the details that impact your business, or you could hire somebody who already has the knowledge.

How to Hire the Right Consultant

You hire a consultant with the same care that you would hire any trusted advisor—very carefully. I suggest that you begin with your existing advisors, especially your accountant. An accountant comes into contact with consultants all the time and very often works hand in hand with them on various projects.

Seek out a consultant with expertise in your industry. A generalist, no matter how smart, does not have the experience that you need. Imagine hiring a consultant for a restaurant who has no experience in the restaurant industry.

Just as I caution you not to trust your instincts too much when hiring an employee, I also caution you not to be in love with your interviewing skills when meeting with a prospective consultant. Get references, and call them. When you interview former or current clients, ask about the results they saw as a consequence of hiring this consultant. A note of caution: the consultant you hire will have experience in your industry, which might mean experience with your direct competitors. Your consultant, assuming he or she is a true professional, will be frank with you about other clients and about issues of competition. If this consultant has worked for one or more direct competitors in your area, this is probably not the consultant for you. Communications with an attorney is governed by the lawyer–client privilege. The lawyer is not only morally bound not to divulge your secrets to a third party, but is legally bound as well. There is no such thing as a consultant-client privilege.

The Consulting Process

Before recommendations comes investigation and study. Your consultant, especially in the early days of the assignment, will virtually move in. No documents should be off limits. A consultant will spend hours interviewing you and your employees. It is critical to alert your employees that you are hiring a consultant, and it's important to enroll them in the process by explaining the benefits of the consulting process. Some workers can be intimidated by the consultant because he or she will be asking them for details about every aspect of their jobs. It's your job to make sure that your employees know that the consultant is on *our* side, not just yours. Let's be frank. One of the recommendations might be that you terminate a certain employee or eliminate the job position. This is a dynamic that cannot be avoided, and it must be handled diplomatically. After many hours of interviews and re-interviews, the consultant will then present you with a written report that analyzes your business, along with detailed observations and recommendations. You might hire the consultant to return on a regular basis to assist you in implementing the recommendations.

Business Coaching: A New Twist on the Consulting Profession

In the last few years, there has been a tremendous growth in the field of *business coaching.* Unlike a typical consultant, a coach is usually a generalist and does not see his or her job as a maker of recommendations, but rather as a facilitator for you to achieve results. Just like an athletic coach, this person's job is to help you perform to your best. A traditional consultant makes recommendations based on the realities of your business and his or her experience with others. A ***coach,*** on the other hand, ***gets inside your head and draws out your own thoughts and ideas.*** Just like the traditional consultant, the coach will first spend a lot of time interviewing you and getting to know you. A major part of the early coaching assignment is to get you to set out your goals because that is why the coach is there—to help you achieve *your* goals.

If you have a goal, for example, of opening up 10 new locations for your business in the next two years, the coach will interpret his job as helping you to get there, after carefully getting you to show the details. A consultant, on the other hand, might simply recommend against the plan based on his prior experience.

A coach can become a part of your business as much as any valued staff member. A coach can be like a partner with none of the negatives or entanglements. A typical coaching arrangement will include weekly phone conferences with an agenda geared to working toward your goals. A good business coach knows every aspect of your enterprise, just like a sports coach knows every play. And just like the sports coach knows who can pull off certain plays, your business coach knows what you can handle and will recommend against a course of action if she thinks you are going in the wrong direction.

More so than in traditional consulting, coaching is a *relationship*. A coach's job is not to be liked, and any coach who tells you what you want to hear is not doing the job. A coach will get in your face when necessary and will confront you with stuff that you won't like. A good coach is aware of your personal nuances and will not hesitate to let you know that you're going off track for a stupid reason. A good coach should also be aware of your personal life and should be attuned to how your life affects your business. She will recognize that an entire session might have to be devoted to your working out an issue about your kid who was just suspended from high school. Until your head is clear of that problem, your business will suffer, and a good coach recognizes this. Finally, a good coach knows that business and life cannot, and perhaps should not, be separated.

And by all means, share the *APT Principle* with your coach. He or she should know that you are using it as a unifying practice for your business and will help you to keep it in the foreground.

Peer Group Advisory Boards: Consulting by Committee

A business peer advisory group is a committee of people dedicated to helping each other resolve issues in their respective businesses. Informal business groups have been around as long as business has existed. These gatherings can be informal meetings in a diner once a week or a formal group organized by a leader who charges a fee and facilitates the meetings.

In 1957, a Wisconsin businessman gathered a group of four other CEOs and started a program in which a member would present issues facing his businesses, and the others would bring their leadership expertise to bear on solving those issues. This group became The Executive Committee, which evolved into the unfortunately confusing name TEC. Saddled with a name that had nothing to do with technology, TEC formally changed its name to Vistage in 2006. Vistage conducts peer groups for CEOs of small and large companies. Another organization that performs a similar function to Vistage is The Alternative Board or TAB.

Vistage is a corporate-run organization that utilizes the paid services of "chairs" who facilitate the group meetings and also provide individual sessions with members periodically. The chair is paid based on the size of the group, which the chair is responsible for forming. The Alternative Board is a franchise and their groups, called boards, are run by franchisees and contract facilitators. TAB also includes not-for-profit executives within their boards and has specific affinity groups, such as manufacturers and attorneys.

I was a member of a TEC group before I sold my business in 2000 and I was then a member of a TAB group, which I joined to help me with new business ventures. Both of these organizations are good, and the concept is sound: business leaders helping business leaders. But there are certain considerations in peer group advisory boards that you should be aware of. The main concern is that group dynamics are at play, and one peer group can be excellent while another can be a waste of time. This is a function of who the members are and how strongly the facilitator runs the program. With a group of 10, a couple of bozos can really screw up a meeting. Fortunately, there are few bozos because the facilitator has a vested financial interest in making the system work and will not allow an obvious jerk to become a member. Both the Vistage chairs and the TAB facilitators are paid based on how many people are in their groups. So, if one jerk causes others to withdraw, that jerk is costing the group leader money.

A typical meeting begins with a light breakfast, followed by each member summarizing his or her month since the last meeting. The facilitator then circulates the *issues* that have been submitted by the members. The first go-around consists of questions to make sure the members understand the issue on the table. Then, each member takes a crack at providing solutions to the issue. Because each member is dedicated to helping his or her peers, the resulting roundtable conversation can be inspiring. While the group is focused on one member's issue, your mind might suddenly come up with a solution for one of your own issues that you didn't realize you had. The discussions can sometimes become emotional, as a member gets clear on an issue with the help of his or her peers. One guy actually began to cry over what we all thought was a simple nuts-and-bolts issue: cash flow and collections. It seems that this fellow gave all of his vendors 60 days to pay, while the standard is 30 days, and it was affecting his cash flow. His emotional response was, as he realized from a sudden dawning, that what he really was doing was avoiding confrontations with people, a shortcoming he'd had since childhood. It's hard to put a price on an experience like this.

Jackie Gernaey is a TAB franchisee from Long Island, New York. During her 11-years with TAB, she has enrolled over 500 business owners in 10 groups with five facilitators. She alone has done over 10,000 hours of coaching for these small business owners. Many of the enrollees stay for over five years. According to Gernaey, "They resolve financial questions, HR, operations, work-life balance issues, and sales and marketing issues. These issues might involve competitive pressures causing eroding margins, reducing the frustration of dealing with employee problems, or getting the business to run without them."

The prices for Vistage or TAB go from hundreds to thousands, depending on the program you select. Both Vistage and TAB provide excellent guest speakers periodically on crucial business topics. Peer group advisory boards can be a powerful part of your business, so it's worth your time to investigate. A potential new member is often asked to sit in on a regular group meeting, an excellent opportunity for the prospective member to see if the reality matches the theory.

Chapter 13 Summary

In this chapter I discussed the following:

- Whether or not to hire a consultant
- How to hire the right consultant
- The consulting process
- Business coaching
- Peer group advisory boards — consulting by committee

CHAPTER 14

Technology to the Rescue

APT Principles: Technology and Practices

The Luddites were a group of nineteenth-century English textile artisans who protested against the changes brought about by the Industrial Revolution. They were known for actually destroying machines, especially looms, which they believed were changing their lives and depriving them of work. There is a theory that the word "sabotage" derives from the Dutch word "sabot," or wooden shoe, and the practice of some workers to throw their shoes into the machinery to cause breakdowns. The movement was named after a mythical figure known as Ned Ludd or King Ludd, who reputedly lived, like Robin Hood, in Sherwood Forest. Today the term Luddite is often used to describe anyone who adamantly resists technology, even though actual machine-bashers are rare. The Luddites yearned for a return to a simpler time and saw the advancing technology of the Industrial Revolution as a threat.

Luddites of today abound, although their numbers are decreasing, no doubt because we are so inundated with high-tech stuff that it is hard to resist its lure. Take the cell phone, for example. If I were to pick out the top five modern marvels that we can't do without, the cell phone would be at the top of the list. It isn't just an instrument of convenience, but it can be a lifesaver. I once spun off the road in a snowstorm, slid down a ravine, and came to a crashing halt next to a drainage culvert. Fortunately, I was uninjured, but I was faced with the immediate task of letting emergency responders know that I was immobile and isolated in a snowstorm. Climbing up the steep snow-covered hill was not an option, at least not a pleasant one. I simply picked up my cell phone and dialed 911. Help was there in minutes. Besides safety, a cell phone can make all the difference when you are expected at a meeting and you are stuck in traffic. The meeting participants are alerted that you may not be there, or will be late, and can change plans accordingly. So, instead of a group of people griping as they waste their time, saying, "Where is that S.O.B.," they know you're on your way, and they have the option to start without you or postpone the meeting.

The value of a cell phone blasts into your consciousness dramatically when you are suddenly without it, and nothing else will do. My wife and I had just gotten off a plane in Turin, Italy, to make a connection to our destination, Venice. I was looking for the men's room, when I suddenly walked through the wrong door and found myself locked out of the disembarkation area. Our cell phone service did not work in that part of Italy. Naturally, my tickets, boarding pass, not to mention my passport, were all with Lynda and the luggage. Airport security measures prevented me from simply finding an open door and walking back in. I had no way to communicate with her, and we had to be on the other side of the airport to catch our connecting flight. My kingdom for a cell phone! Fortunately, I was able to plead my case to a security cop, who spoke fairly good English. I explained that if we missed our flight, my wife would kill me. He got it. He flagrantly violated the rules and let me back in. I love Italians. I couldn't even write a letter of commendation to his bosses because he probably would have been fired for allowing an American jerk into the security area without a passport. But the experience reminded me how this modern convenience—which came into popular use in the early '90s—became an instrument that is essential to our lives. Occasionally, I meet someone who actually does not own a cell phone. One cell phone-free person I know is a newspaper reporter. I'm not making this up. She shares a distaste for spending money on technology with her boss, the publisher, who is too cheap to spring for a phone for every reporter. "How," I asked, "can the editor get in touch with you when there is a breaking story, and he needs you to be on location?" The procedure was for her to call in every few hours to see if there was a breaking assignment. Stuck in the '80s!

It's becoming quite rare to encounter a person who doesn't use a cell phone. But people who don't use e-mail are more common. Like you, I have served on or chaired many charitable committees, and still do. It seems that almost every committee or board I serve on includes one member who does not use e-mail. When I am in charge of the committee, the solution is simple. The person either gives me the e-mail address of someone he sees often, who can then print out and hand him e-mail correspondence, or he simply gets off the committee. When such a person says that I should simply mail it to him, my response is always this: "Let me get this straight. I send out an e-mail to everyone on the committee, but you want me to stop what I'm doing, print out the letter and an envelope, address it and put a stamp on it, and bring it to the post office so that you can mail me back your response that I need within a matter of hours?" "But can't you just call me?" asks my Luddite friend. So, instead of hassling with written correspondence, I face the prospect of my day being interrupted by having to place a call, possibly get involved in phone tag, and then go through the totally unnecessary small talk when I finally make contact. Technology deniers need to understand the needless crap that they inflict upon technology users. **Attitude** meets **technology**.

Am I Talking About You?

This book is written for a business of any size. If your business has more than one employee (you), I am going to make the wild assumption that you have adopted at least part of the modern technological revolution; otherwise, you would have an extremely hard time finding your first employee. But I have met people who think that technology is for employees to use, to free you up for the really important matters. This is erroneous thinking of a major dimension, and I suggest that you take a look at your **attitude**. I actually knew a guy who had his secretary do all his Internet research—not just some, ALL. He would not Google his own questions for fear that it might take him away from his big thinking. Now, I'm not suggesting that a large research project has to be done by you, but the answer to most quick questions is right there at your fingertips.

Computer "Illiterates"

I still meet people, some in responsible positions, who say, as if it were a matter of pride, "I'm computer illiterate." If this is you, get a grip! Being computer illiterate today is getting pretty close to simply being illiterate. I'm a fairly polite person, or at least I try to be, so when somebody tells me he or she is computer illiterate, I don't ask, "Are you insane?" But I do engage the person in a conversation about technology-avoidance, and I'm amazed that the anti-tech person usually has the same narrative to explain why he or she doesn't use technology, and the defense is wrapped in philosophical terms. The narrative is usually a variation of one of the *following excuses:*

Why learn? "I have employees, so why do I need to learn to use a computer?" If you're comfortable with having your employees be knowledgeable about a huge part of your business, you should get out of your comfort zone.

I am old fashioned. "I prefer to do things the old way, with a personal mailed note, a phone call, or a meeting." A personal, hand-written note is a wonderful thing and, yes, it does jump out because it is so rare. I'm not at all against it, for limited use such as a thank-you note or certainly a condolence card. But consider that an anti-tech person is always two to three days later than the rest of the communicating world. Phone calls and meetings have their place, but a good manager has to decide if a simple e-mail communication might be better. This is no hard and fast rule, but don't assume the party you're dealing with shares your enthusiasm for time-consuming methods of communication.

Computers waste time. "People who use computers waste a lot of time. I'm free!" There is some truth to this, which I will address shortly. Keep in mind that people waste a lot of time in traffic when they could be galloping along the shoulder of the road on a horse.

Technology is too expensive. The most expensive part of your profit and loss statement is payroll. To the extent that you make your employees more productive by giving them the proper technological tools, your bottom line will improve.

I'm too old to learn this stuff. Nonsense! You need not learn *all* the stuff but enough to make you a productive manager. It's never been easier to learn about computer use and other tech gadgets. YouTube, the amazing Google-owned website of video clips, has an enormous number of free video lessons on all sorts of technical matters. Lynda.com, to which I subscribe, is a fee- based online university where you can take lessons on virtually any aspect of computer usage and the necessary software. So don't worry; you didn't miss the boat. It has never been easier to learn about computers. The "old days" of the early '80s were different. The weird old days of MS-DOS are gone forever.

Technology Changes Faster Than Ever

I am writing this book in the spring of 2012. Not long from now, a lot of what you are about to read will have changed. A few years ago, all the chatter, from Silicon Valley to Wall Street, was the search for the "Killer App," the software application that would create a shift in the way we do things. My first computer in 1982 was a TRS-80 Model II. TRS stood for Tandy Radio Shack. It didn't use MS-DOS, the *M*icrosoft *D*isk *O*perating *S*ystem, but TRSDOS, for *T*andy *R*adio *S*hack *D*isk *O*perating *S*ystem. It had 64 K (that's kilobytes, not megabytes or gigabytes) of RAM or random access memory. The first Killer App I bought was indeed a killer: VisiCalc, the world's first commercially available spreadsheet program. As a publisher of periodicals, accounting practices required that I record a thing called unexpired subscription income, meaning that I had to spread the income for each subscription payment over 12 months. From a bookkeeping perspective, this was one huge pain in the butt. VisiCalc was a Godsend. I actually convinced my accountant that he should get it and use it. VisiCalc is the grandfather of Excel, Microsoft's wonderful spreadsheet program. The other Killer App was a word processing program called Scripsit. Our old IBM Selectric typewriter suddenly looked like a museum piece. Even almost 30 years ago, I noticed the productivity enhancement that the computer provided. Back then I couldn't have imagined what the technology explosion would mean. The Internet was a thing known only to a few scientists. We haven't seen the last of the Killer Apps. I just read about an app that you will soon be able to download to your smartphone that will direct you to an empty parking space in a crowded city. Killer!

So the discussions and suggestions in this chapter will have a relatively brief shelf life, but that's not a problem. Publishing is going through its own technological paradigm shift. As I discussed in the chapter on writing, books can now be produced using the new technology called one-off publishing, meaning that it can be as cheap to create one book as to produce a thousand. This makes a big difference to publishers and authors because new editions are easy and cheap to produce. This bodes well for academia, business, and society as well because old, obsolete books will be updated with current information.

The Primary Business Needs for Modern Technology

What follows in this section is similar to "Top 100" lists. Some magazines have stopped publishing Top 100 lists because the entries on the list are entirely subjective. Please read this section with that thought in mind. These are *my* observations and suggestions, and it is by no means infallible. Over the years I have been a journalist, lawyer, publisher, and author. I know my way around technology, but I am not an oracle. That said, let's take a look at what your business needs from technology, at least as I see it.

Communications

I discussed the cell phone, now bundled with a PDA into a smartphone, and how it has changed the way we do things. But telephones, or telephony to use a high-tech word, are only a part of the space we call communications. How your business lets the outside world know about you, whether the issue is marketing, customer relations, or customer support, is something that requires a strong working knowledge. Some of these software solutions have been discussed elsewhere in this book, so I shall not repave the same road.

E-mail

It might seem strange that this technology, which I have discussed often, reappears here. But it is such an important, constant part of your regular communicating that I am going to drill down a bit farther and offer a few tips that, in my experience, can save you a lot of grief.

When to use it and when not to use it. Professor Nicholas Negroponte, in his groundbreaking book *Being Digital* (First Vintage, 1996), drew a distinction that I think is critical when thinking about communication. I also discussed this earlier in the chapter on time management. Should the communication you are about to have with someone be synchronous (necessitating a give and take), or should it be asynchronous (where the back and forth between people is not necessary). "When should we schedule the Annual Dinner?" This will require a lot of input and ideas from all involved, so it probably should be a synchronous communication in the form of a meeting or a conference call. But "Please be in my office for a staff meeting Tuesday at 9:30 a.m." is asynchronous: you're telling somebody simply to be there—no discussion is necessary. This is easily handled by e-mail. Amazingly, Negroponte's book is not available as an e-book in digital format.

Reply and reply all. If you take this to heart and learn the critical difference between these two buttons, you may save your business, stay out of a lawsuit, and generally avoid a lot of ugly mayhem in your life. This applies especially to a large organization, which, thanks to e-mail, may be geographically diverse. A message sent to a bunch of people might contain some information about which you have a strong opinion. If you express your opinion to "all," you can run the risk of seriously alienating some people for no good reason. A regional manager named Bob sends a message to everybody in a group of intended recipients. One of the group sends you a direct e-mail (not to all) indicating his displeasure with Bob. Instead of just replying to him, you reply TO ALL that "Bob is a flaming idiot." Whoops!

Re: Re: Re: Re: Re: When sending an e-mail message, always change the subject line to convey the subject of the message you are sending. Some people, many people, through simple laziness, just hit forward, reply, or reply all to send a message that has absolutely nothing to do with what they are communicating in the current one. A couple of years ago, someone in our vacation condo association sent out something about parking spaces. To this day, I get e-mails with the subject line saying, "Re: Parking spaces" that have nothing to do with parking spaces.

Don't be a comedian. Use humor, if you must, but be appropriate. A poke in the ribs in-joke might work in the hallway but looks weird a few years later in an old e-mail. What seems funny when spoken can come across very differently in an e-mail. Be really careful when using humor at someone else's expense.

Do not EMWD! What, you may ask, is EMWD? It is e-mailing while drunk. If you have had a few pops too many and are feeling loquacious, unplug your computer. What seemed to you like beautiful prose that evening might be horrifying when you read the response in the morning. This rule also applies to EMWA (e-mailing while *angry*). When we used to communicate by paper mail, the tasks of printing out the letter, signing it, putting it into an envelope, and putting a stamp on it provided a lot of waypoints for rethinking the message we were about to send. The good news is that e-mail is fast. The bad news is that e-mail is fast.

DO NOT SHOUT! What you just read is called SHOUTING, the inappropriate use of capital letters. It's okay if you want to EMPHASIZE SOMETHING, but it is completely tacky if this is your default font when writing anything. It makes you look like an amateur, especially when you're SHOUTING about something that is not worth shouting about. It also eliminates your ability to emphasize something that you really want to stand out. Twitter and Facebook, for example, have no bold, underline, or italics, so all caps is the only way to EMPHASIZE a word.

Break up your message into bite-sized paragraphs. If you want your e-mail to be read, put yourself in the place of the reader. Appropriate use of paragraph breaks is always a good rule of writing, but it is critical when using the Internet. People expect punchier messages on the computer screen. We live in the Information Age, and we all share the responsibility to deliver information as efficiently as possible. A never-ending paragraph screams out, "Don't read me!"

Use a signature. All e-mail software programs enable you to put in a signature or contact information automatically when you begin a message. Why everybody doesn't do this stumps me. You can even use different identities, for example, one as the head of your business, and the other showing you as a member of a not-for-profit board. Sometimes your message will result in a return phone call for clarification. Unless your contact information is there you are forcing the recipient to look up your phone number. If nothing else, a signature line with contact information is a simple courtesy. Not only do you make life easier on your recipient by having all your contact information right on the message, but a signature also provides you with a valuable *branding opportunity*. In any e-mail program, instructions on how to add a signature are usually found in *preferences* or *options*. My emails, for example, have my name and under it my position as editor of my blog The Moran Report, along with the web address phone numbers and so on. Every time I send an email, it's a branding opportunity. It's simple. Just do it.

Make nice. E-mail has become such a dominant part of our everyday communication that obeying rules of etiquette simply makes sense. An excellent and well-titled book on the subject is called *Send: The Essential Guide to Email for Office and Home* by David Shipley and Will Schwalbe (Knopf, 2007).

E-mail Marketing Services

These services didn't exist just a few short years ago. Once, you had to work around your regular e-mail program and do the best you could. These programs are a very effective way to help get the word out about your business. You can create and monitor professional e-mail marketing campaigns, which allows you to announce news, tell your subscribers about new products or services, send out advertisements, or announce special events. In some cases, you can also send out surveys to get valuable feedback. Like anything, it takes some time to set up and think through, but once done, you have a highly automated way of keeping in touch with your customers and potential customers. These programs pay careful attention to the unsubscribe feature, automating the way people can opt out of your e-mail blasts so that you don't run afoul of statutes that bar unsolicited e-mail blasts. In my observation, Constant Contact seems to be the big gorilla in this marketplace, owing perhaps to its own excellent marketing. I attended a free e-mail marketing and social networking seminar put on by Constant

Contact, and I was very impressed by the knowledge of its presenter, Ellen DePasquale. Constant Contact's E-mail Marketing tool is really a one-stop-shop for all your e-mail marketing needs. From customizable e-mail templates and seamless list management to social sharing features and integration with your blog posts, Constant Contact's offerings could take up an entire chapter. My wife uses Constant Contact in her work as director of an arts council, and I use it as well. I do not hesitate to recommend it. It's one of those software solutions that make life a bit easier. But Constant Contact is not the only player in the space. Others are iContact, Benchmark Email, Mailpen, Pinpoints, Campaigner, GraphicMail, Mad Mimi, Vertical Response, and MailChimp. For reviews and rankings, see www.toptenreviews.com.

Blog Services

I discussed the blog as a marketing tool in Chapter 12. It is here in the technology chapter because you need the right software to make it happen. A blog, or weblog, is a good marketing tool to get the word out, provided you like to write or are willing to hire someone who can. There are some very sophisticated software programs for you to make this happen. WordPress is by far the major player in this market. I use WordPress for my blog, *The Moran Report*. WordPress naturally touts itself as being simple. It is, to a point, but once you hit a snag, getting out of it can be maddening. There is no help desk; you are directed to a forum of other people who you hope have an answer to your question. But it is, as advertised, a very complete and powerful tool. The others in this business are TypePad, Squarespace, Blogger, Myspace (remember them?), AOL Journals, Windows Live Spaces, Xanga, and LiveJournal. For comparisons, check out www.toptenreviews.com. But unless you commit yourself to a regular schedule of blog posts or have someone to do it, a blog will be a total waste of your time. That said, it's a great tool.

The Smartphone

What has become known as a "smart" phone is really a cell phone that does a lot more than handle phone calls. With my Blackberry, as just one example, I can check or send e-mail, send or receive text messages, look up a date or schedule an event in my calendar, look up or insert a contact, and entertain myself with cool games while waiting in line at the supermarket. I could write an entire chapter, even a short book, on the subject of a smartphone, but the market place for these devices is changing so rapidly that it wouldn't make sense. What does make sense is this question: Do you have a smartphone and, if not, why? These devices enable you to carry a significant part of your business on your belt or in your purse. For a business person in today's world, a smartphone belongs in the definition of *no-brainer*.

Online Meetings

This is where technology has taken a simply amazing turn. A typical business meeting for a company of any size that is not located in one building or within a short travel distance involves a lot of time and money. Besides the air-fare, hotel prices, and meals, there is the unavoidable fact that travel time is not productive time. Although it may be bad news for the travel industry, the personal computer can now take the place of a sit-down meeting. GoToMeeting (www.gotomeeting.com) enables you to have a meeting with a group of participants right on each user's PC screen. It even enables you to have high-definition videoconfer-encing when you want to have face-to-face contact. As of this writing, it will cost you $468 per year for a maximum of 15 attendees or $4,788 for up to 1,000. Compared to the cost of flying, boarding, and feeding a bunch of people at a central location, this is pocket change.

Filing

This subject might seem too boring, especially because you, the manager, seldom get involved in filing, except for your own desk area. Please read on. You won't be bored. There is no hard and fast rule that determines where stuff gets filed, although secretarial schools have recommended methods. The fact of life is that each person in your office who files things uses his or her intuition. There is a document from Allstate Insurance Company that needs to be filed. Does it get filed under Allstate or insurance, casualty insurance, or roof dam-age claim? Some people, out of a desire for excess cau-tion, make copies and file it in various locations. This is a waste of time and effort, and it creates a potential for confusion. The problem jumps front and center when employees leave because they take their filing philoso-phy with them.

Technology to the rescue. You can either scan each document and have an electronic database of searchable stuff; or use a system of keywords. The problem with scanning is that a good high- speed scanner is expensive and, for digital searching, you are at the mercy of the current state of optical character recognition—one smudge, and the document may never be retrievable. I use a software product called The Paper Tiger and have done so for many years, ever since I sold my company. The concept is simple, and the execution is even simpler once you've set up the system. Setting it up can take a few days depending, of course, on the size of your enterprise. Each piece of paper gets put in a *numerical file,* and there is no special meaning attached to the number. Before you put the paper in the file, you enter *keywords* on the software screen that corresponds to the numbered file that will enable you to locate the document in seconds when you want to retrieve it. In the example above, the Allstate document would get the keywords Allstate, insurance, casualty insurance, roof damage claim, and perhaps the name of the broker or claims adjuster. When you enter one of those words into a search box, the file number appears. Before I sold my company, I had staff members who would worry about filing paper, and I never thought about it. I discovered something about myself: I have no talent for filing. Even though I no longer owned a company, I still had all sorts of business and investment interests to keep me confused. I would put everything into a large box with "to be filed" written on it. Guess what? The stuff never would get filed. When the time came (and it came every day) to retrieve a document, I realized that my non-filing system was becoming a big problem. I saw an ad from the Paper Tiger people promising to eliminate filing problems. I'm always skeptical of ads, but I was a prime target because I needed help desperately. I was not disappointed. The software has become a mission-critical part of my technological arsenal. I couldn't do without it; I'm a writer, not a paper-looker-upper. They also have a new product called Digital Tiger, which organizes all the digital files on your computer. Check it out at www.thepapertiger.com. They even provide you with a list of consultants who will come to your place of business and, for a fee, handle the transition process.

Computer Systems

Whether you should use Windows-based computers or Macs is a subject beyond the purpose of this book. If I could state a general rule of thumb, it would be that graphics-intensive businesses tend to use Macs. For some reason, Windows-operated computers have become known simply as PCs, even though a Mac is clearly a personal computer. Any time you call tech support for any product, the first thing you are asked is, "Are you using a PC or a Mac?" If I were limited to emphasizing one point on the subject of computers, it is this: they eventually break down or become obsolete, and to the extent that you try to keep an old computer working, when in truth it just wants to roll over and die, is the extent to which you are committing a very Bad Practice. Technology is all about making your business perform at its peak level of productivity. When you push an old system beyond its useful life, you are sucking productivity out of your business for the sake of trying to save a few bucks. Note that I say "trying to save" because you are not saving money when a high-paid employee, or you for that matter, spends part of every day trying to tame gremlins that infest an old computer. Buy or lease a new one.

Good financial management means building up cash for necessary purchases. Replacing old equipment should be a regular **practice,** and a painless one if you have the cash to do the job. The equipment has probably been depreciated down to nothing, so you won't get a tax deduction by donating the stuff to a charity, but you should donate it anyway if you can find some organization willing to take it. Some organizations have volunteer geeks who raid old computers for parts.

Proper use and management of technology will keep your business on the cutting edge. Would you rather be the cutting edge or the chopping block? Your call.

Chapter 14 Summary

In this chapter I discussed the following:

- Being a tech avoider
- Technology changes faster than ever
- The main business needs for modern technology
- Communications
- E-mail
- E-mail marketing Services
- Blog services
- The smartphone
- Online meetings
- Filing
- Computer systems

CHAPTER 15

Should You Buy a Business?

APT Principles: Attitude and Practices

The question of acquiring another business to complement or expand your existing one cannot be reduced to an easy formula. We'll look at valuation formulas later but, for now, you must answer a few questions before you even begin to look for a business to buy. If you do go down the acquisition road, your accountant and attorney will have hundreds of questions. But first, you'll need to come up with some general answers:

Do you really want to expand your business by acquisition, or do you simply want to keep adding customers and clients to grow what you already have? In other words, how fast do you want to grow?

Does an Acquisition Make Sense? Are You Unique?

Is your business so unique that an acquisition wouldn't make sense? There are some businesses that are so specialized that they thrive on simply managing what they already have. Take, for example, nuclear security consulting. There are not a lot of those guys around. Simply trying to be the best is probably an excellent plan, and acquisitions might not make sense. **Attitude** check: you need to apply a lot of imagination addressing the issue of uniqueness. Although your business may be unique, there might be areas for expansion without producing a negative impact on the way your business works, or without damage to your brand. In the 1970s, consumer products giant Clorox bought the charcoal briquette maker Kingsford. It then purchased the familiar synthetic fireplace log company Duraflame. Say what? You can't use synthetic logs in your barbecue, and you can use charcoal briquettes in your fireplace. One of the major reasons for the acquisition, besides a desire for product diversification, was that Duraflame logs would tie up supermarket shelf space in the winter, and the Kingsford charcoal would take over the summer. Imagination can lead to synergy.

Could your business expand into another type of business without disrupting your existing operation? I knew a guy who had a successful oil delivery business with hundreds of customers. He eventually bought a burglar alarm business and made a tremendous success of it. Now what do oil and burglar alarms have to do with each other? Besides water, I can't imagine something that goes less with oil than burglar alarms. But here is what my friend knew: he was buying locations and customers, and that's what the two companies had in common. His task was to simply convince his existing (happy) customers that he was the guy to provide for their security needs as well. So, he bought a book of unrelated business, and it gave him the opportunity to sell burglar alarms to his oil customers and oil to his newly acquired security customers.

Will an Acquisition Disrupt Your Current Operation?

Is your existing business mature and running smoothly and with healthy enough cash flow to handle the inevitable disruptions of an acquisition? That's right—I said the *inevitable disruptions* of acquiring a business. I grow ill when I hear about a seamless integration performed with flawless execution. Baloney! Doesn't happen here— maybe in Oz. And by the way, Oz doesn't exist. I'm not saying there aren't good acquisitions; there are, and there are great ones. But speed bumps come with the game, and sometimes the game is nothing but bumps. AOL and Time Warner? How's that for seamless? Hewlett-Packard and Compaq? How's that workin' out for ya? Mergers and acquisitions are not for kids, at least not for stupid kids. But knowing that there will be problems, the issue before you is whether your existing operation can handle the big changes ahead.

Is your acquisition target a direct competitor, the revenues from which will now flow from it to you? There are a lot of truisms and aphorisms in the world of business, and you will often hear this one: "It's easier and cheaper to buy a business than to start one from scratch." And like all truisms, this has a bit of, well, truth. The obvious fact is that the business is there; it has customers, revenues, employees and, one hopes, profits. The business took years to build, and it's now a going enterprise. But the big question for you is this: Should you buy a business or just keep building on what you already have? Is it really cheaper to buy what's there than to build your own?

The Value of a Business: Formulas are a Starting Point

Every business has a value, and that value can be put into a range of numbers that is surprisingly objective. Just like appraising a house or determining the value of an injury in a lawsuit, sales of businesses have left behind a trail of history over the years, and that historical trail results in some interesting averages that can be reduced to formulas; and those formulas provide a sparkling gem: a reference point to begin negotiations. A formula might say that in your industry, the typical selling price is nine times the average of the last three years' net earnings. But that doesn't mean that the price for the business you are interested in buying is a simple arithmetic sum derived by plugging in the numbers on which the formula is based. It's not quite that simple. Comparable sales in real estate, for example, might indicate that a four-bedroom, three-bathroom house on a half acre in a certain neighborhood is worth $500,000. But much more goes into it, and that's what real estate appraisers are for. These folks use a form, which you probably have seen, that includes many variables that add to or subtract from the home's value. The appraiser will add or subtract amounts based on the home's condition, age, views, and a host of other amenities, like central air conditioning, a swimming pool, a new furnace (or an old one), a new or old roof, and various other value-comparing points.

The valuation of a business is more complicated. Again, assuming that the objective historical value of a particular type of business is nine times the average net earnings over the past three years, the negotiating table could really have a big banner hung over it which reads, "Why should this business go for more (or less) than the nine times net formula?" The negotiation will then proceed with the seller trying to show why it's worth more, and the buyer trying to show it's worth less.

Buying a Business is Seldom a Do-it-Yourself Exercise

Donald Trump isn't shy about touting his skills as a negotiator, but then, Donald Trump isn't shy about anything. But unless you are like Donald Trump, I urge you to put a skilled negotiator between you and the other party. Negotiating is a learned art, but part of it is innate, something that's in your gut. Some people love the give and take of making a deal, much like a tennis player who loves making a good shot. But even if you are a skilled negotiator, you should consider that having someone represent your interests is, in itself, a negotiating strategy. Your representative has the ability to slow things down at the appropriate moment. Suppose the seller says to you, "Here is my final number." You are then left with two options: accept the number, or try to convince the seller that further discussion is necessary. Your representative doesn't have this problem and will tell the seller that he will have to discuss the number with you. He will let a couple of days go by and then contact the buyer and say, "I think we may be close." It's an intricate dance, which, performed correctly, avoids toes being stepped on.

Everything in this chapter also applies to the next chapter about selling your business, except from an obviously different point of view.

Chapter 15 Summary

In this chapter I discussed the following:

- Expanding by acquisition or by continuing on your own.
- Does an acquisition make sense?
- Will an acquisition disrupt your current operation?
- Formulas as a starting point in calculating the value of your business.
- Buying a business is seldom a do-it-yourself exercise.

CHAPTER 16

Selling Your Business

APT Principles: Attitude and Practices

Unless you intend to have family members take over your business, you are eventually going to look for a buyer. You have spent years building your company, and now it's time for what may be the largest financial transaction of your life. But before we look at the intricacies and the strategies of selling, we have to look at some basic issues before you go to market.

Do You Want to Sell Your Business?

If your business is fulfilling your life both financially and personally, selling might not be a great idea. There is no possible way that I could make a recommendation here, even if you and I knew each other personally. I knew a guy who owned a large insurance agency. At age sixty-five, he was a fireball of energy, and his enthusiasm for his business seemed boundless. Nevertheless, he decided to sell and retire and do something he dreamt about all his life—he became an archaeologist. This is a decision that only you can make, but I suggest that your decision whether or not to sell should be the result of taking a hard look at reality.

Your age and health. Even if you had not thought about selling, your business plan should include the critical component of *succession planning*. I'm assuming here that your plan is not to have family members take over the business, so succession planning is really another way of asking this question: Are you prepared to take care of your family without the business? If you were suddenly out of the picture, would your spouse be able to run it? Would he or she want to? This is where the conversation necessarily turns to estate planning.

Market timing. If your familiarity with your industry tells you that the future looks rough, maybe you should ask yourself if you want to be a part of a tougher business climate. The flip side of this coin also lands in the same spot. If business is booming, perhaps you should take advantage of the boom by selling into a hot market. Look at the home construction business or any business having to do with real estate a few short years ago. People who had well-polished crystal balls sold in 2005. How is your industry, and where is it headed?

Are you tired of your business and looking for a new, exciting adventure, or are you simply ready to retire and smell the roses? If so, the obvious answer is to sell. There might be openings in archaeology.

When Do You Prepare to Sell Your Business?

The answer to the above question is *right now*. That's RIGHT NOW. Before you question the sanity of what I just said, consider the following. I had no intention of selling my company in 1999. I didn't even think about it. It wasn't that I would never consider selling; it was just that I was having fun and making a lot of money, so why should I consider stopping the music? But one day I got a phone call from the CEO of a large publishing company who said he would like to have lunch with me. I will go into more detail on this later, but the point I am making is this: sometimes a buyer shows up when you least expect it. Opportunity sometimes knocks. Are you prepared to answer the door? The payoff of putting the principles of this book into reality is that your business will be in great shape at any time, ready to show to a potential buyer.

Steps to Selling a Business

Hiring the Right People to Help You

As I discussed in the chapter on buying a business, having someone else in the negotiating process is, in my opinion, crucial. First, look to your existing advisors. Is your attorney or his law firm experienced in M&A (Mergers & Acquisitions)? This is a complex specialty, and you should have a frank discussion with your lawyer. I'm not suggesting that you go out and hire an expensive (and they *are* expensive) M&A specialist right away. But if you do, keep your contact with the attorney to a minimum until you have found a buyer, and limit your discussions strictly to legal questions. The hourly billing can add up fast. There are M&A consultants who are similar to high-priced business brokers but provide expertise and guidance way beyond simply finding a buyer. An experienced M&A consultant will work hand in glove with your attorney when the time comes. Because M&A consultants get paid a fee based on the sale, you do not rack up big legal fees in the beginning of the process.

Your M&A consultant should be the person you do most of your communicating with. He or she will guide you on "going to market" and has the incentive to get you the most money because his fee is based on it. M&A is a game. M&A people know how to play it and win.

Research and Analysis: Who Wants to Take You to the Prom?

Working with your consultant, you will start your journey by researching the primary candidates, or types of candidates, who may be logical buyers for your business.

- Is it a direct competitor?
- Is it a competitor, but in a different market area?
- Is it a company that could grow rapidly if it acquired you?

Think synergy. Is it a company, perhaps from a different industry, that could acquire your business as a strategic asset? Remember the discussion in the previous chapter about Clorox buying synthetic log maker Duraflame to tie up supermarket shelf space to complement its Kingsford charcoal business? Also, remember my oil delivery friend who bought a burglar alarm business so he could market a new service to existing customers? If there is ever a time to think outside the box, this is it.

- Is the candidate company publicly held and traded on a stock exchange? Publicly held companies bring something special to the game: publicly traded stock. The price tag on a purchase paid with stock can often be huge. SEC requirements have strict rules on how much of the stock of the acquiring company you can sell in a given period, but don't be concerned about your lifelong nest egg being tied up on the stock in one company. Without getting too complicated, you protect your downside by purchasing a derivative security known as a put. When you own a put on a stock, if the price goes down, you make money.

The Dance Begins

Your consultant or broker begins the process of escorting you to the marketplace of businesses for sale. He will use a multifaceted approach, including ads in the *Wall Street Journal*, Internet postings, word of mouth, surveying contacts in the industry, and generally getting the buzz going. Experienced M&A consultants or brokers have a well-developed list of contacts to whom they can drop subtle suggestions that they know of a company for sale. Good brokers are networkers, enabling you to tap into their network. They often earn their fee based on their contacts alone.

Getting You All Dressed Up for the Initial Presentation

Attitude. Your M&A consultant first needs to learn everything about your business. After all, you are the product he or she has to sell. Your M&A person will spend hours and days with you, getting inside your head, learning first about your attitude. That's right, *your* attitude. What, you may ask, does your attitude have to do with selling your business? Everything! Your M&A person wants to know if you have the toughness to go through the arduous rounds of negotiations, and just how much you are willing to bargain to transfer the business to the seller. Your consultant wants to know if you are really willing to walk away from the table if an acceptable deal can't be struck. There is an old saying in the art of negotiating, and it has everything to do with attitude. "If you can't walk, you can't talk." If you are willing to call off negotiations that are going nowhere, this attitude, and that of your advisor, will show during the talks.

Practices. Your M&A consultant wants to know everything about your Best Practices and expects you to be blunt where some of your practices are anything but *best*. This becomes part of his or her sales presentation to a prospective buyer and the buyer's advisors. Think of all of your practices as a PowerPoint presentation because that's exactly what it will become. Going through every aspect of your business and showing how your practices have made a powerful contribution to its success makes for a very compelling presentation. Depending on your skills as a presenter, you both may agree that *you,* not the M&A consultant, will make the presentation to the buyer. This is usually done in a formal meeting where the buyer and his advisors will be sitting there with one basic question: "Why should we buy you?" When I sold my company, my M&A consultant and I determined that I would make the presentation. I had many years of public speaking experience, so it made sense. I can't determine if this is the best course of action for you because the decision is based on your experience. Caution: some people—maybe you—are more impressed with their own perceived sales ability than the person on the other side of the table might be. A few years ago my wife and I were shopping for a new house. We found one that really appealed to us. When we went to the showing with the broker—a very experienced salesperson—the owner cleared his throat and delivered a non-stop speech about the splendors of his dwelling, following us around to see if we had any questions, and basically making such a pain in the ass of himself that we couldn't remember the details of the house after we left. We didn't buy the house. The point is this: work with your consultant to see if you or the consultant should make the presentation.

Technology. This is part of your initial presentation along with Best Practices, but you need not go into excruciating detail, which will be left for the due diligence phase if the deal moves forward. The purpose of showing the technology aspects of your business is to demonstrate to the buyer that you are using every resource available to you and that these resources add to the value of your business. Here, as elsewhere, it is important not to exaggerate or to gloss over deficiencies. If your network needs upgrading, say so. The buyer wants to know, if he turns the key, that this thing is going to start.

Anatomy of a Deal

No two business deals are alike, but there are certain waypoints or deal components that are usually present. The details, of course, will vary, but there is a general outline of what any deal looks like.

Non-Disclosure Agreement. It's in both party's interest that the negotiations remain strictly confidential and that even the fact that discussions were held should not be made public. If the deal does not happen, the buyer doesn't want you to discuss the negotiations with another party that the buyer might want to acquire. Likewise, as a seller, you don't want the details leaked to another potential buyer.

Initial meetings. During the initial meetings, a lot of general knowledge about your business is disclosed to enable the buyer to decide if it makes sense to go forward. For good reason, both sides usually want the other to come up with a price. The buyer wants to know if the seller is going to be reasonable, and the seller wants the same from the buyer. In the sale of my company, the buyer flatly insisted that we come up with a price. Since the deal would stall if we didn't put a number to it, we agreed to go first, and my attorney hit the buyer with an absurdly high price, one that I couldn't justify by any manipulation of the numbers. But it didn't kill the negotiations; the buyer's acquisitions team decided to move to the next phase with their own numbers in mind.

Letter of Intent. This is not a binding contract to sell your business but, as the name implies, an expression of the buyer's intent, subject to due diligence and the seller's disclosure of every detail asked. It's as though the buyer said, "Okay. If you can show us this and that, here is what we would be willing to pay."

Structure of the Buyout

Cash. This is the best for the seller because once the deal is done, it's done.

Stock or stock and cash. If the buyer is a publicly traded company, this is a common deal. If however, it is closely held, it can be a different story. A closely held company is one that does not sell its shares to the public through an exchange. The stock in a closely held company often has no value because there is no market for it, and the value turns into money only when the company is sold. Notice that I say often, not always. Facebook, which is a closely held company, probably won't go public until the end of 2012, but investors, as of the fall of 2011, have valued it at over $80 billion. If Mark Zuckerberg offered to buy your company *now* for shares of Facebook's closely held stock, I suggest that you listen intently. It depends on the acquiring company. The company that bought mine was closely held, but it was owned mostly by a private equity firm. Private equity firms are deal makers, not folks who love to run businesses. It was clear to my advisors (and me) that they would eventually look for a buyer. Therefore, I accepted stock options as part of the sales price. They had no value at the time of the sale in 2001, but when the company that acquired mine sold to another company in 2007, the value I received from the exercise of the stock options was almost 10 percent of the entire deal. So, stock or stock options can be an excellent offer, depending on the company making the offer.

Earnout. An earnout, or a limited earnout with some cash up front, is usually the worst deal for the seller.

As the name implies, the price for your company is partly dependent on your earning it by staying on board and hitting minimum performance criteria. A deal like this can make sense for the seller if there is a significant amount of up-front cash, and the seller realistically believes he or she can hit the financial criteria. A situation like this often comes up when there is an impasse on the price. For example, the buyer is adamant that he is willing to pay no more than $5 million and you, the seller, are equally adamant that you want $8 million. Assume that the buyer's offer is not far off based on actual performance of the business in the past. By including a $3 million earnout based on objective financial goals, the buyer is protected because if you don't hit the goals, you don't get paid. And you are taken care of if you have been realistic and are able to hit the goals. An earnout agreement can often close a deal that has stalled.

Employment agreement. It's very common for a buyer to want you to stay aboard for some time to ease the transition, to answer questions, and to show the new owner how the business works. In any given deal, depending on what your personal efforts brought to the business, the buyer may want you to stay on as the head of the company, which will now be a division of the acquiring company. In effect, you will have cashed out but still remain as the CEO with a handsome salary. It's impossible to cover the rainbow of possibilities that cover your involvement in what was once your business.

After the Deal is Done

If you stay with the business in any capacity, you will suddenly find yourself in a strange place. It might be the same building you formerly occupied and you might sit in your same office, but *you are no longer the boss.* You might be the titular head of the new division, but you suddenly find that you are no longer the one calling the shots. The success or failure of the acquiring company's relationship with you and the employees is almost totally dependent on **attitude,** theirs and yours. The new owner is certainly entitled to have things run its way—it's their company. But how the new managers manage *you* can make or break the success of the company. Are you a team player willing to separate your former ownership from your feelings about your former position? Can you be open to new ideas, including **practices** and **technology,** from the buyer? If you find that you hate the new regime, and want out, your contract should have a clause enabling you to do so. But, of course, you will forego your salary. If the salary is substantial, and you don't want to give it up, your only option is to make the best of the situation and soldier on.

The most important thing is this: You've cashed out. You've turned the business that you grew into a liquid asset. If you have worked your business plan and have used the *APT Principle* to keep you on track, you now have the ability to look forward and do some more planning. The big difference is that now the fun part of planning takes front stage. It's time to smell the roses, or maybe take up archaeology.

Chapter 16 Summary

In this chapter I discussed the following:

- Deciding whether to sell your business
- Preparing to sell your business
- The steps to selling your business
- Hiring the right people to help you
- Research and analysis
- Getting you all dressed up for the initial presentation
- Non-Disclosure Agreement
- Initial meetings
- Letter of Intent
- Structure of the buyout
- After the deal is done

CHAPTER 17

Conclusion

There is no such thing as a self-executing plan any more than there is a plan that writes itself. Planning is the most dynamic process that you will ever encounter, and the reason it's dynamic is that it occurs during a timeline of reality over which you have little or no control. So, if planning, both the writing of it and its execution, is so dynamic, why plan at all? Just manage the dynamic stuff that smashes into your face as it happens. A lot of businesses do just this, and a lot of stuff gets smashed into a lot of faces.

Planning is a must because it gives you the blueprint, including your **attitudes, practices,** and **technology,** to help you to cope with and conquer the dynamism of life. This book is meant to be read, to be used, and to be a part of your business plan. As you have seen, each chapter includes a summary of what the chapter was all about. I suggest that you keep this book handy and refer to the chapter summaries from time to time; better yet, consider this book like a time-gnat. If you think about reading it, you will think about how you should be applying its principles. Once that thought enters your head, it will become one of those little incompletions that rob you of time—a time-gnat. So kill the gnat by writing it down, and schedule a review of this book at regular intervals.

If this book has altered your thinking on business planning and the process that goes into it, it will have had a dramatic impact on your business. And if that happens, I shall have succeeded.

Please feel free to contact me at russ@morancom.com. I am also on Facebook and Twitter.

May your plan fuel your dreams.

About the Author

Russell F. Moran was the founder and CEO of Moran Publishing Company, Inc., best known for its weekly *The New York Jury Verdict Reporter*. The company also published *Judicial Review of Damages,* a monthly that published what happens to jury verdicts on appeal, and the *Civil, Criminal, Matrimonial and Tort Citators*, books that were updated quarterly and are used by lawyers to prepare motions and appeals. The company sold in 2000. He has appeared on TV and radio and has been quoted in numerous publications on jury trends, including the Op-Ed page of *The New York Times*. Moran is an attorney and the author of *Justice in America: How it Works—How it Fails.* (Coddington Press, 2011). He graduated from Chicago-Kent Law School, where he attended with a full academic scholarship and served as an editor of the *Chicago-Kent Law Review.* In his senior year he taught legal research and writing. He has consulted with small businesses CEOs on startup practices, business planning, and market optimization, using the tools of *The APT Principle*.

He lives on Long Island, New York with his wife Lynda and his Shih Tzu Sammy.

Index